THE EVERYDAY ENLIGHTENED COOK

Low Calorie, Fast and Easy Cooking with Reduced Fats, Salt and Sugar

BETTY CARR

KEY PORTER BOOKS

To my children, Candice and Michael. They have always been a source of great encouragement during the writing of this book. I thank them for their eager efforts as taste testers.

And to my mother, who taught me all the basics in the kitchen, and so much more.

Canadian Cataloguing in Publication Data

Carr, Betty, 1947-
    The everyday enlightened cook

Includes index.
ISBN 1-55013-358-6

1. Low-fat diet — Recipes.   I. Title.

RM237.7.C37 1992   641.5'638   C92-094509-8

Illustrations: Laura Kendall
Typesetting: Computer Composition of Canada Inc.
Printed and bound in Canada

Key Porter Books Limited
70 The Esplanade
Toronto, Ontario
Canada M5E 1R2

92 93 94 95 96 6 5 4 3 2 1

Contents

Preface

Armed with a great deal of knowledge and years of experimenting and cooking in the style represented by this book, I set out to create a cookbook dedicated to that style and to everyone who loves to eat.

North Americans have become increasingly aware of the health risks associated with diets high in saturated fat, sodium and sugar. These items have been used in excessive amounts for many decades, both in the preparation of food at home and in prepared foods, including that from fast-food outlets and restaurants.

There seems to be no lack of information on the harmful effects associated with the excessive use of fats of all types, sodium and sugar. There has been some more recent information pointing to possible health risks with high-fat diets in general. Though conclusive studies are still under way, we are being encouraged to reduce all fats to a level of 30% of our daily calories. Always follow your doctor's and/or dietitian's recommendations about how much to reduce your intake of fats, sodium and sugar.

The recipes in this book use foods that can be found in most grocery stores across the country. There are no exotic or unusual ingredients. All recipes using eggs have been tested with whole eggs, part whole eggs and whites, and only egg whites. Which you choose will be a matter of personal diet monitoring. Including fiber in your daily diet has a proven value to good health, and many of the recipes use fiber in its many forms. Though I am dedicated to reducing fats of all types, sodium and sugar, this would be of little use if the food didn't taste sensational, and it does.

I developed many of these recipes over the last 20 years. They have become family favorites. Others I specifically developed in my kitchen, sometimes referred to as my laboratory. Food, special diets and the relationship of physical and mental performance to the food we eat have been lifelong interests of mine.

My very first adventures in cooking started when I was around six or seven. That is when I pushed a chair up to the counter to see what my mother was doing. It didn't take long before I had my hands into things and became first assistant baker. By the time I was into my teens, I was changing and converting many of my mother's recipes. I was almost thrown out of home economics class in Grade 7 for refusing to make cookies with lard.

My children urged me to write a cookbook. After looking over the available cookbooks and observing many people, the food they eat and the methods they use to cook that food, I became convinced that the average person had better get serious about changing his or her eating and cooking habits.

I am really pleased to be able to share with you my experience in low-fat cooking. I hope these recipes will become your favorites, too.

Included is some of the latest information on cholesterol, sodium, sugar and fiber as well as important consumer data that will help you make wise choices in the grocery store. There is information to assist in streamlining preparation time, and included are methods geared to preserve the nutritional values of the food being cooked.

You will find the approach here to reducing fat, sugar and salt to be a practical and common-sense method that will suit any life-style. It is not radical or time-consuming.

We are moving into a whole new age of understanding the relationship of the food we eat — how it can increase our performance levels and work for us, too, as preventive medicine — and long-term studies have given new emphasis to healthy eating. The 1990s will see the beginning of some real changes that will revolutionize the processed-food industry, as well as our own kitchens. There's no doubt that the time is right to examine and improve our own eating styles.

Getting Started on a Low-Fat Life-Style

If you have not yet changed your diet to reflect the latest medical advice to lower fats of all types, or if you have not been able to maintain a healthy weight, the following information will assist your efforts. These methods apply equally well to cooking and eating.

Easing into a low-fat diet is easier if you gradually change your eating habits. At the same time that you reduce your intake of fat, the sources of sugar and salt will also be reduced, since both are usually used to excess in a great many high-fat and processed foods. Learn which foods are naturally high in fat, and read labels to identify the products that use excessive fats of all types.

One of the greatest sources of invisible calories is fat. Many products contain an unhealthy excess of fat. At the top of this list are baked goods — cookies, crackers, cakes and muffins, to name just a few. Even if these fats are unsaturated (see "Understandings Fats", pg. 17) they still contain the same amount of calories as saturated fats, and it is all types of fats — from any source — that should be reduced.

To start, examine your own daily and weekly eating habits. Review the foods that you regularly prepare at home. Many may be easily trimmed of excess or unnecessary fat.

Reducing — or, better, eliminating — visits to fast-food outlets is another good way to start. And if you're eating out, do not be fooled into thinking a salad with dressing is a healthy meal, for the dressing contains enormous amounts of fat. At home, switch to the new no-fat dressings now available in most grocery stores, or make your own. Dairy foods have undergone many changes over the past few years. We are seeing low-fat cheeses, yogurt and milk. Since milk and milk products are a good source of calcium, they still play an important role in a nutritionally balanced diet. Substitute the new lower-fat dairy products, and keep consumption to sensible amounts. Dairy products *can* be part of a low-fat diet.

The number of egg yolks you eat should be carefully monitored if you have high cholesterol levels. Even if you do not have this problem, you should realize that the yolk is a source of fat. Reducing the use of yolks is a sensible way to control fat consumption. In the chapter "New Eggs and Cheese" there are many innovative ways to reduce yolks. When eggs are used in any recipe in this book, yolks are reduced in number or, wherever possible, eliminated.

Processed foods of all types have become part of our everyday diets. Avoid all products that contain tropical, palm or coconut oils (saturated fats) and products that have a high fat content of any type. Processed meats are loaded with fat, salt and long lists of chemical additives. Seek out alternatives: cold homemade meat loaf or roast beef sliced thin.

Trimming fat from meat and poultry, choosing extra-lean ground meats and reducing the quantity of meat consumed will aid in an overall fat-reduction program. The consumption of foods that are high in fat, such as bacon and pork in general, should be reduced then removed as a regular item from your diet.

Since we now spend a great deal of time eating away from home, learning how and what to order in a restaurant will also help you reduce fat intake. Avoid cream soups and cream pasta sauces. Instead of traditional creamy salad dressings, ask for a dressing of fresh lemon juice, vinegar and granulated garlic. Do not hesitate to ask for your chicken to be grilled without the skin, or to ask for the fish without the cream sauce. Always request that vegetables be steamed and served without sauces or butter. Avoid sour cream on a baked potato. If you cannot live without the sour cream and low-fat yogurt is not available, choose a different vegetable. All fried foods should of course be avoided.

Review your regular use of all added oils and fats in your everyday cooking. The foods in this book are cooked with a minimum of fats. Where necessary, only enough is used to achieve the appropriate results. In baking, fat is crucial to produce a good product. Bake a pan of homemade low-fat cookies; to prevent over-eating, bake only half the dough; freeze the rest for another time.

Take a tour of your kitchen and read the labels of the products you normally buy. Check out products in the grocery store, acquaint yourself with the healthiest available and keep current on new products. Food producers are bending to consumer demands.

About the Ingredients in This Book

All the ingredients used in these recipes can be found in most grocery stores. Availability may vary from place to place, but for the most part if something is not available, an appropriate substitute can usually be found.

I use the word "appropriate", for in substituting you should consider your own dietary requirements. Products that contain high amounts of salt, sugar and fats should be avoided or monitored within reason. Just as we have counted calories in the past to avoid ingesting too many, we must now learn to monitor and control the amount of sugar, salt and fat we consume. The key here is to achieve a proper balance.

All the recipes in this book were created to eliminate excessive amounts of salt, sugar and fats that most recipes have contained in the past. Increasing fiber also became an important consideration to overall healthy eating. In doing this, I was also able to reduce the calorie count.

Decreasing the use of processed foods and replacing them with fresh is one of the easiest ways to reduce much of the salt, sugar and fat that have crept into the average North American diet over the past few decades. With so many women having joined the work force in recent years, I also had to address the issue of time. Meals today have to be fast and easy to prepare.

In these recipes I have used products that are currently the best available on the market. From time to time, improved ones will be introduced in stores. When that happens, it would be prudent to start using these new ones. Be advised that the use of eggs is kept low, and where possible all or some of the yolks are eliminated.

When oils or fats are used — and this is kept to the lowest level possible — I have recommended certain types as being the best, according to the latest findings. Keep in mind that "low cholesterol" doesn't mean low fat or calories. Therefore, the amount of oil being used is very restricted, and wherever possible not used at all. For baked goods, I have used margarine as the solid fat. This seems to be the best choice at the moment when a recipe calls for a solid fat. However, margarines are not all the same, and there is a constant stream of new types. Check out the section in this book called "Understanding Fats" for how to make the best selection in the store.

We are on the threshold of a new era of food. The processors are listening. New products reduced in salt, sugar and cholesterol are finding their way to the grocery shelves every day. Many processors have announced plans to alter formulas to conform to the growing demands of consumers. Keep yourself informed of all the changes.

Adding Fiber to Our Diet

In the past decade we have seen many new cookbooks specializing in high-fiber diets. Food manufacturers have also increased the use of oats, multi-grains and other fiber foods. According to the latest research by Health and Welfare Canada, in the "Report of the Expert Advisory Committee on Dietary Fiber" (1985), the consumption of commercially produced products will not produce the health benefits we have come to expect from fiber-containing foods. Increased fiber has been shown to have a direct effect on metabolizing the foods we eat as well as on disease and other chronic conditions. Certain forms of cancer have been linked to low-fiber diets.

One clear message comes through: we should increase fiber in our diet. The best way is to include food naturally rich in fiber. To simply define where these wondrous fibers are found would be to say they are of plant origin — vegetables, fruits, grains, beans and nuts. (Nuts are high in fat, though, so do not eat them too often.)

Since the type and quantity of fiber will vary with each source, it is wise to include a variety of types to produce maximum benefits. In their natural state plant foods are rich in fiber. When these foods are refined, however, they lose some of their fiber. Polished rice and white flour are among the most common items that have had fiber content decreased by the refining process.

Increasing fiber should be approached in a sensible way. *Gradual* introduction or increase of high-fiber foods will allow your digestive system to adjust and will not cause you any gastrointestinal problems.

A sensible eating plan goes hand-in-hand with wise choices at the grocery store. Fresh and unrefined foods supply a full quota of fiber as well as essential vitamins. Include and increase vegetables and grains at each meal while reducing animal-source proteins. (This is also important for overall fat reduction.)

Salt in Our Diet

Salt is hidden in almost everything we eat, both naturally and added. Generally, the naturally occurring salt is in minor amounts compared with processed and pre-prepared foods. Always keep in mind that processed foods do contain large amounts of added salt. That is why processed foods are unacceptable for most sodium-restricted diets and certainly not recommended on a regular basis for the rest of us.

In the past few years, some food processors have made an effort to produce lines of sodium-reduced products. This has been helpful; however, read the label. Do not be misled by the words "reduced salt"; the product may still contain a high amount of sodium. As informed consumers, we can make ourselves heard by the food processors. The results are now evident with the number of new "reduced salt" products available.

Even for those people not on sodium-reduced diets, a little moderation in the use of added salt in cooking, at the table and in processed food will go a long way to reduce the health risks associated with the overuse of salt. Discover how herbs and spices create new taste sensations.

In this book, salt has been reduced but not entirely removed. The products that were used in testing were considered for their salt content, and overall salt quantities were considered.

Over the years, as our lives have become busier, the amount of fast foods and processed products consumed by all of us has dramatically increased. Salt is a cheap additive that gives flavor to processed food and helps reduce bacteria. Estimates from numerous sources indicate that most North Americans get the majority of their salt from processed foods.

With an average recommended amount of between 1100 mg and 3300 mg of sodium per day for healthy people, where does that put your lunch today? A Burger King double beef Whopper with cheese contains 1535 mg of sodium. Add regular french fries at 230 mg (onion rings are 450 mg), a vanilla milkshake at 320 mg, and the lunch totals 2085 mg of sodium. To further make your day, the calorie count for the same meal is 530 for the Whopper with cheese, french fries 210 (onion rings 270), milkshake 340. The total is 1080 calories. Look at these numbers carefully if you're trying to lose weight. The percentage of fat is also out of line with today's healthy standards. (Although here I zero in on Burger King, no matter which fast-food outlet you eat at, the numbers are about the same.)

Getting a Handle on Salt

Reduce your salt intake by cutting back on the largest source: processed foods. Replace the processed foods with fresh. Fresh tastes better, has excellent nutritive value, and much of it can be prepared quickly.

Eating out can be a problem only if you see it that way. Many restaurants offer fresh foods cooked to order. Learn what to order in restaurants: salads to replace salty soups; fresh lemon, oil and vinegar dressing, or granulated garlic and vinegar; and baked potato with yogurt and freshly ground pepper make great replacements. Be creative. Variety and new tastes await you.

Also at the restaurant, the salt shaker can be replaced with your own blend of herbs and spices. Carry your own reclosable shaker filled with your favorite blend. The use of condiments should not be excessive, as they contain large amounts of salt.

How Sweet It Is

Sugar! We all try to reduce the use of white granulated sugar in our diets, for many reasons. Whatever the reason, do you know what type of sweetener is in the food you eat?

Let's start with some basics. If better nutrition is your reason for seeking an alternative to white granulated sugar, many excellent choices are available: honey, molasses, treacle, maple syrup, corn syrup, sugar cane syrup. Nutritional values aside, these alternatives are real sugar. That means they raise your blood sugar quickly and will contribute to tooth decay.

Other sweeteners that are sugars include dextrose, glucose, sorghum, lactose, maltose, levulose and fructose. As a general rule, when you're reading the package watch for ingredients ending in "ose". This will help you to spot a form of sugar being used.

Watch for the catch-all "nutritive sweetener" description. This includes sorbitol, manitol and xylitol. They are all forms of sugar. Nutritive sweetener refers to a form of sugar that contains calories and raises blood sugar levels quickly. Non-nutritive sweetener refers to a group of sweeteners that do not contain calories and do not affect blood sugar levels.

Non-nutritive sweeteners unfortunately have some limitations and possible risks that prevent them from being used in all food products. Cyclamate, first synthesized in 1939, is 30 times as sweet as white sugar. Its use was banned in Canada and the United States after it was found to cause cancer in laboratory animals. No evidence of cancer was ever found in humans. Cyclamate is still being used in more than 40 countries, and there is much public demand in the United States to lift the ban. The Food and Drug Administration is currently evaluating petitions for approval.

Saccharin, first made in 1979, had limited use. Many users noticed a metallic aftertaste. Saccharin was removed from the market when studies using laboratory animals showed a higher incidence of bladder cancer. The American Medical

Association has stated that saccharin appears safe and should remain available.

Aspartame was discovered in 1965 and was approved for use in 1981 in dry products and in 1983 in soft drinks. As a food additive, in the form of NutraSweet, it has virtually no calories. Its granulated tabletop form, Equal, contains some dextrose and dried corn syrup. Each packet (equal to the taste of 2 tsp [10 mL] of sugar, which contains 32 calories) has 4 calories. The main advantage of aspartame is that it tastes very much like sugar and has no metallic aftertaste. Its main disadvantage is that it becomes unstable when heated. Equal cannot be used in cooking. Like other artificial sweeteners, aspartame came under suspicion in cancer studies but has been cleared in recent reports.

Anyone concerned with the safety of any sweetener should take it in limited doses. In fact, one of the more reasonable approaches has been to combine sweeteners. The sweetening effect is stronger than the effect of either one taken alone. This means that only very small amounts of each sweetener are required, and it ensures that you will ingest an amount of any sweetener that is well within safe levels.

Added sugar in one form or another is a large part of our diet in the world of prepared, packaged and fast foods. Learn to read labels, and know that the hidden sugar consumed every day far outweighs the teaspoon added to a cup of coffee.

Awareness is the answer. What does it mean when we see packages labeled "light", "no sugar added", "calorie-reduced" or "dietetic"? The only way to determine sugar and fat content is to read the label. Never assume that the product has no sugar. Manufacturers have been allowed to use these misleading labels, and we have been so ready to believe them. For the most part, manufacturers of these "no-sugar" products have replaced the traditional white sugar with dextrose, lactose, sorghum, maltose and an ever-growing list of sugars disguised with various names. This is not to say that all products contain added disguised sugars, but be aware that they can.

If you feel that spending your life in a grocery store reading every label is a somewhat fanatic approach to a sensible diet, you may have a point. However, if you are diabetic, hidden sugar is not something to overlook. And for everyone, knowing what you are eating should be a primary consideration. Better public awareness will in turn force realistic standards upon the food industry.

A Special Note to Diabetics

All the recipes in this book may be used as is by diabetics *except in the baking sections.* These baked-goods recipes may be used with the following change: Reduce all the sugar by half and substitute an amount of artificial sweetener to equal the eliminated sugar. Where brown sugar is used, a brown sugar substitute will simulate the flavor.

The amount of sugar used for yeast doughs need not be adjusted, as 1 or 2 tbsp (15 to 25 mL) will not present a health problem.

Understanding Fats

It seems everywhere you turn today, people are talking about fats. Manufacturers are labeling everything "No Cholesterol". With some products this label is being misused, since the product never contained cholesterol to begin with.

In many products the manufacturer has replaced the heavy saturated oils once used with very good polyunsaturated or monounsaturated oils. This has been a great step forward for all of us. Do not become confused, however. There may still be some small amounts of saturated fat in the product, in the form of hydrogenated oils. Hydrogenated oils are to be avoided.

Saturated fats are found naturally in many foods. The latest findings have suggested a healthy maximum of 30% of daily calorie intake should come from oils and fats, with no more than 10% as saturated fat. Dieters take note: removing excess oils and fats from your diet can tip the scale in your favor.

Fatty acids, which make up a large part of the fat in foods, can be separated into three categories: saturated, monounsaturated and polyunsaturated.

Though we should restrict all fats, the saturated fats are the ones to reduce from the levels most of us are now consuming. They are easy to detect, as they usually have animal origins. Common examples are lard, chicken fat and suet.

Vegetable oils, made from plants, are monounsaturated and polyunsaturated, and should be the oils of choice when oil is used.

Canola oil is sold in Canada in all major grocery stores under house-brand labels, and in the United States under the Puritan label. Canola is considered a better choice because of its high percentage of monounsaturated fat and its low level of saturated fats. It outranks corn, safflower, sunflower and soybean oil. Many recent studies have shown it to be the best vegetable oil on the market today, ranking alongside olive oil. Olive oil is also monounsaturated, and it has recently regained popularity in North America.

NOTE: The exceptions to the plant-origin oils are palm and coconut oil. Often called palm, palm kernel or tropical oil, these are extremely high in saturated fat and should be avoided. Check out those packaged cookies and crackers and all processed foods before you buy them. You may find these tropical oils listed along with the other ingredients. In response to growing pressure from the public, some manufacturers have started to remove the palm and coconut oils.

Spreading the Word on Butter and Margarine
Butter, as we know, is a saturated fat and should be avoided by anyone on a cholesterol-restricted diet. For those who want to use butter and reduce calories and cholesterol, try the recipe on pg. 35 for Soft Whipped Diet Butter.

Your decision to use or not to use butter is a simple one, and it depends upon your dietary requirements. This is not such a simple matter when you turn to margarine to replace the saturated butter. The margarine you choose may in fact be no healthier than butter.

All margarines are not equal. A chemical process called hydrogenation (adding hydrogen to fats) turns vegetable fats that are fluid at room temperature into fats that are solid. This is the common process that makes solid margarine and shortenings from liquid vegetable oils. However, hydrogenation also turns monounsaturated and polyunsaturated fats into undesirable saturated fats. It gets even more complicated when manufacturers use more than one type of fat in the margarine blend. This can sometimes be a saturated fat like palm or coconut oil.

If you combine a saturated fat with hydrogenated vegetable oil, depending on the overall ratio, the margarine may not be much better than butter in cholesterol content. Read the label and check for tropical or palm oils. Check for the percentage of hydrogenated oil, which is sometimes stated as a percentage of the overall oil. (The smaller the percentage the better.) If it is listed in the ingredients it should be placed low on the list, since ingredients are listed in order according to the amount used.

What to Look For

The differences in saturated fats among stick, soft tub and liquid margarines can be small. Look for a margarine that lists a liquid oil as its first ingredient. Go for a low percentage of hydrogenated oil, and stay away from those that list palm or tropical oil anywhere in the ingredients.

A new generation of margarines is now available on the market. The overall saturate level has been reduced, we are seeing calorie reduction, and there are soft margarines. These soft margarines may be easy to spread, but most are not recommended for use in cooking and baking. The ingredients added to create softness and calorie-reduction alter the chemical structure needed for successful baking and cooking. (See recipe for Soft Whipped Diet Margarine, pg. 36.)

Since canola oil was introduced, I have been waiting for a margarine made from this wonderful product. One has just come to market in Canada, and I have tested it extensively. It is a soft-tub type and reduced in calories; it works perfectly well in all baking and cooking. It does, however, contain sea salt, and so it should be avoided by people on sodium-restricted diets. (Maybe we will see a salt-free version soon.)

Hydrogenation and saturated fats do not stop here. The supermarket shelves are loaded with processed foods that contain hydrogenated fats and/or saturated tropical oils. Be aware and read labels. Manufacturers are listening to consumers, and some have changed or are planning to change their formulas. (As a note of interest, many of the manufacturers are replacing the tropical oils with canola oil.)

The Best Is Yet to Come

The prospect of eating fried foods, regular salad dressings, ice cream and more without the fats and calories usually associated with these products sounds too good to be true. Yet a number of fat substitutes will soon be on the market.

Olestra, from Procter & Gamble, is defined as a sucrose polyester. Soybean oil is its main ingredient. The chemical structure is changed so that the body's enzymes, which break down fat, do not recognize Olestra; it therefore passes through the body without being absorbed. More good news is that Olestra has the same taste and cooking properties as regular oils and fats. Procter & Gamble is awaiting approval for this product. Olestra will be used to replace part of the oil in numerous products.

Simplesse, by the NutraSweet Company, was announced in January 1988. This product is quite different from Olestra, being made from whey protein or egg whites. It will be replacing ingredients that in the past were not just fats but contained cholesterol as well. Simplesse will be limited to use in cold products, since it cannot be heated. Salad dressings, mayonnaise, sour cream, ice cream, yogurt, cream cheese and processed cheese spreads will contain it. Simplesse has been approved for use in ice cream and is becoming more widely available.

A number of large companies have developed similar products now waiting approval from the Food and Drug Administration in the U.S. From this a whole new generation of foods with lower levels of fat will emerge to help us maintain a healthy diet while enjoying our favorite foods. It is expected that these new products will have a great influence on the fast-food industry, food processors and our own kitchens.

The Use of Oil in Cooking

Most of us try to reduce or eliminate saturated fats in our diets. Recent health studies have shown that all fat should be restricted. Many health care specialists have recommended that no more than 30% of our daily intake of calories should come from oils and fats, with only 10% being saturated.

All kinds of claims have been made that excessive amounts of fat in general can cause many types of illnesses. Though evidence to substantiate these claims is not conclusive as yet, there are some real benefits to a fat-reduced diet. Fewer calories and weight reduction are among a growing list.

Aside from knowing the best oil to use for the purpose of general cooking, we must also consider calories. Even unsaturated oil has an abundance (120 calories per tablespoon), and so the use of it should be restricted.

Many methods of preparing food do not require the use of oil. Consider not using any oil for cooking and small amounts of flavorful oil as a condiment, much the way spice is used. Added at the end of the cooking time, a very small amount will go a long way to add flavor.

Most of the oils sold in Canada are highly refined and deodorized, and for the most part are used to cook food and to grease pans. Unrefined oils have fragrance and taste, complementing and enhancing food.

The rich aroma and nutty flavor of sesame seeds, almonds, walnuts, peanuts and the fruity taste of olives are all available in oils to enhance a variety of foods. As a general rule, the aromas and flavors of these oils are best at room temperature. You can cook with them, but in most cases their distinctive flavor is lost when they are heated. This is good news, for all that is needed to enhance flavor after the cooking is a very small amount lightly brushed over the surface or added to a sauce. When unrefined oil is well made, it has the taste and aroma of whatever it was made from. If poorly made, it can taste bitter, harsh or bland and tasteless. When the oil becomes rancid it has an unpleasant flavor. These oils should be refrigerated, or they will go rancid.

Olive and most nut oils, including canola, are of vegetable origin and contain monounsaturated fatty acids.

Olive Oils (unrefined)

Choosing a good olive oil does not have to be complicated. Check the label first. Extra virgin oil is made from the choicest olives. The oil is extracted using no heat in the first pressing of the olives; this is called cold pressing. Heat is then used to extract additional oil. This oil from the second pressing is called virgin olive oil, superfine olive oil or fine olive oil. The third pressing is called pure olive oil, and is made from the pulp after the second pressing, and lower-quality olives are sometimes used.

Manufacturers sometimes mix pure olive oil with a quantity of higher-grade olive oil to give it better flavor. "Pure" on the label means no other type of oil has been used.

Italian olive oil is considered by many to be the finest in the world. This oil is very rich, with full olive flavor and a deep, almost emerald color. French olive oil is delicate with a sweet fruity flavor and is light golden. Spanish oil has a strong olive flavor and a thick consistency, while Greek oil is thick with a lighter olive flavor.

Since extra virgin olive oil is expensive, it is a waste to use it in complex sauces and recipes having many ingredients. Likewise, high heat and prolonged cooking can destroy the delicate flavor. Very small amounts can be added to cooked sauces, or a small amount might be lightly brushed over steamed fish or chicken. Try small amounts of this oil mixed with well-aged wine vinegar over a salad.

Virgin olive oil (second pressing) seems to be the choice for general cooking purposes. It's lower in cost than the first pressing, but with reasonably good flavor.

Sesame Oil (unrefined)

The intense scent of roasted sesame seeds is the aroma of a good sesame seed oil. Only a few drops can add wonderful flavor to many foods. The thick brown oils from China and Japan have the richest flavor. Oils from other parts of the world are light in color and far less aromatic.

Rethinking our use of oil and reducing its use can be of great benefit. Pan sprays have always been the choice of dieters; their use also restricts the amount of oil added to whatever is being cooked. Using surface-coated pans and cooking liquids as oil substitutes are two of the ways we can all reduce our oil consumption.

For the most part, using oil in cooking needs a whole new set of rules. Most of all the key is to use it sparingly, if at all.

Flavors and Seasonings

The types and combinations of flavors and seasonings available to us are quite staggering. Learning how to use and combine flavors will bring your cooking to new heights. Pure flavors can be in the form of extracts or flavorings that are made directly from the substance. These two forms vary only in strength. The extract is pure, highly concentrated and expensive. The flavoring is pure, less concentrated and less expensive. Some flavorings are produced from artificial ingredients; avoid these because the small saving in price is not worth the inferior taste.

The most common and universally used extract is vanilla, but many other extracts have great potential. Pure forms of almond and lemon are usually available in grocery stores; others in the fruity category may be harder to find. Next time you are in a liquor or wine store, browse in the liqueur section. This is where to find some of the most exquisite pure forms of flavor available today. (In the long run they are also very inexpensive, since the flavor is highly concentrated and only small amounts are used at a time.)

Peach, orange, lemon, apricot, mint, chocolate, strawberry and raspberry, just to name a few, are all available as liqueur or brandy. A bottle of inexpensive brandy should be as much a kitchen essential as vanilla. If you do not want to use a brandy or liqueur (even though the alcohol cooks off with heat), substitute extracts are available.

Extracts will work well in many recipes in place of the source ingredient. For example, almond extract can replace almonds — a good alternative when you're calorie-counting. A small amount of apricot brandy can turn sautéed chicken breasts into an extraordinary feast. Alcohol evaporates when the cooking temperature is above 175°F (80°C), so there is no need to worry about the alcohol remaining in the soup or a batch of cookies.

It was mentioned in the "Understanding Fats" section that small amounts of very flavorful oils can be used for flavoring. When they are added at the end of the cooking period, they retain their full flavor.

As a rule, ingredients that contain intense flavors need only be used in small quantities. This can work well if you are following a fat-sparing diet. As well, very small amounts of strong cheese can in many recipes replace large quantities of less flavorful cheese. Always buy the strongest Cheddar available, use less in cooking, purchase low-fat cheeses and enjoy all the flavor — with reduced fat.

Spicing It Up
Pure spices are easily available. Buy only the freshest. When spice is exposed to heat or air, it loses potency. How it is packaged for sale as well as the way it is stored at home will determine its ability to do a good job for you. Store spices only in tightly closed containers away from heat (that is, not above the stove, next to the refrigerator or in direct sunlight).

Never buy any one spice in enormous quantities; even packaged well, spices have a short shelf life. Some recommendations suggest storing spices for no more than one year. I feel that some spices lose potency sooner. Use the sniff-and-taste test to determine the condition of your spices. Writing the date of purchase on the container will also help.

Never buy garlic salt or onion salt. What you are getting is a lot of expensive salt and not much spice. Granulated garlic and granulated onion (which are pure) are similar to instant coffee granules that have been ground a little finer. The aroma is that of fresh chopped, and the flavor is fully released when the granules are mixed into moist ingredients. Granulated garlic and onion can easily replace fresh when you are in a hurry or didn't make it to the market. The recipes in this book may be made with fresh garlic and onion or the granulated type.

Herbs are wonderful and add a touch of magic to many foods. Many enthusiasts grow fresh herbs in little pots in the window; others grow them in the garden then dry bunches for use year-round. These herbs are the most flavorful, but for us rather hurried people, fresh are now showing up in grocery stores. When you have fresh herbs, freeze or dry what you don't use. Frozen or dried herbs work well in cooking, but frozen herbs are not ideal as garnishes. I must confess that although I like to use only fresh herbs, this is rarely possible with my hectic schedule. I keep a small supply of my favorites dried in tightly closed jars.

For each 1 tbsp (15 mL) of fresh herbs, substitute 1 tsp (5 mL) dried, or ½ tsp (2 mL) crushed, or ¼ tsp (1 mL) powdered. Delicately flavored herbs should be added only near the end of cooking time. Never use too many different types at the same time, and go easy on the amount being used.

Suitable types and amounts of herbs are recommended in the recipes in this book. If you have little experience with herbs, start by purchasing one or two. A good way to learn the flavor of an herb is to use only a small amount in a soup, stew or casserole. Discover your favorites, and experiment.

Spicing and flavoring can come from many sources: even the distinctive combination of the foods that cook together, the vegetables that are added and whatever else may come to mind. From time to time, items are added to the cooking food that will not actually be eaten but do impart flavors.

A common example is the bouquet garni. It's made up of small amounts of herbs tied into a small piece of cheesecloth or filter paper. The flavor cooks into the food without the herbs themselves becoming part of the food. Some other favorites include bay leaves; a thick slice of fresh horseradish, caraway seeds tied in cheesecloth, and parsnips and bones with meat for soups. (Do not throw away that stripped turkey carcass; put it in a pot with water and cook up a flavorful broth, which can be a base for any type of soup.)

A number of Season All blends are available in the grocery store. Each spice company produces its own blend, but they are all similar, containing a variety of spices.

Onions, green and red peppers, chili peppers, celery, garlic, green onions, to name a few of the more popular, all enhance with wonderful flavor.

Flavoring is a matter of personal taste. If you prefer, adjust the amounts of herbs and spices given in these recipes. Also keep in mind that food served hot requires less spicing than food served cold.

I encourage you to experiment with flavor. When the meal tastes great, nobody will miss the fat, salt and sugar.

Anytime Snacks and More

Pita Pizza

Perfect for a snack, fast lunch or dinner. Vary the ingredients according to your taste and to what may be available in your refrigerator. (Leftovers work well, too!) Prepare in quantity, wrap each in waxed paper and freeze 4 to 6 in a plastic bag. Heat one in a toaster oven or several in the oven. For individual pizzas, each 6- to 8-inch (15 to 20 cm) pita round should be cut around the edge to separate into two rounds.

Half	pita (try oat bran)	Half
2 tbsp	tomato sauce (or tomato paste thinned to sauce consistency)	25 mL
	Granulated garlic	
	Granulated onion	
	Mixed Italian herbs	
	Sliced mushrooms (optional)	
	Thinly sliced pepperoni or very lean wieners (try a very lean-type turkey, veal or chicken)	
2 to 3 tbsp	shredded skim-milk mozzarella	25 to 50 mL

On each inside side of the sliced pita half, spread the remaining ingredients in the order given. (At this point, the pizza may be wrapped and frozen for later use.) Bake pizza in 450°F (230°C) oven until cheese is hot and bubbly. The toaster oven can be used to make 1 or 2 pizzas. Serve hot. Makes 1 pizza.

Variations:
The following toppings may be used as substitutes or in combination: thinly sliced tomatoes, chopped eggplant, chopped sweet green or red pepper, chopped broccoli, fresh sliced mushrooms, sliced olives, almost any leftover vegetable, thinly sliced zucchini, chopped washed fresh spinach, or any sliced or chopped cooked meat.

Hearty Meat Pizza
Substitute Barbecue Sauce (pg. 64) for the tomato sauce and omit the spices used above. Use cooked crumbled extra lean ground beef, chicken or veal. (Any leftovers will do.) Add vegetables and skimmed-milk mozzarella. Bake or freeze as above.

Note: Hard vegetables are better precooked and chopped small, as the pizza cooks for only a short time.

Crystal Chicken Pita

Try this for a snack or dinner on the run. The chicken can marinate for half an hour or all day in the refrigerator.

2 tbsp	cornstarch	25 mL
1 cup	water	250 mL
3 tbsp	Kikkoman low-sodium soy sauce	50 mL
2 tbsp	dry white wine (optional)	25 mL
1 tbsp	sesame seed oil	15 mL
1 tsp	granulated garlic	5 mL
1 tsp	granulated onion	5 mL
4 to 6	chicken breasts, cut in ½-inch (1 cm) chunks	4 to 6
2 to 3	pitas (each 6- to 8-inch/15 to 20 cm)	2 to 3
	Shredded lettuce	
	Chopped tomato (optional)	

In bowl, mix cornstarch with water. Stir in soy sauce, wine, oil, garlic and onion. Add chicken. Marinate for at least 30 minutes.

Drain excess liquid off chicken. Heat a non-stick pan; pour chicken into pan. Cook, stirring constantly, for 4 to 5 minutes.

Cut each pita in half to form 2 pockets. Place a layer of shredded lettuce into each pita pocket. Fill pita with chicken and chopped tomato (if using). Makes 4 to 6 half pitas.

Bagel Thins

These cracker-like thin slices have been showing up in many stores. I have been making these for many years without the addition of oil, spice or preservatives. Spices can, however, be · used if you want. I use an electric food slicer to get an even and very thin cut from the bagel. It can be done by hand, but it is hard and the results are not as good. Whichever way you slice them, try to start with day-old bagels because they slice better when they are not fresh. For variety, look for different types of bagels: white, black, marbled, plain flavor or with herbs or spices. They are wonderful with anything on them for a snack or meals instead of a slice of bread. They make great open-faced sandwiches.

6 to 12   day-old bagels

Assemble the electric food slicer and slice each bagel; adjust the slices so they are very thin but not paper-thin. Place bagel thins on several cookie sheets. Bagels can be piled 3 to 4 layers thick.

Place in 350°F (180°C) oven, turning and shifting bagel positions from time to time to ensure even doneness. The browning time will vary depending on the amount of bagels being done at one time.

Store in a closed container or plastic bags. Makes about 40 to 80 bagel thins.

Crisp Bread

This crisp cracker-like flatbread is very easy to make. Do not be surprised to see it disappear quickly. Great with all types of spreads or eaten plain. It makes a beautiful presentation on an appetizer tray.

2½ cups	all-purpose flour	625 mL
½ tsp	salt	2 mL
1 cup	warm water	250 mL
1	egg white, beaten	1
2 tbsp	water	25 mL

Toppings:

Black pepper
Caraway seeds
Dill seeds
Dried herbs
Garlic
Italian herbs
Onion
Parmesan cheese
Poppy seeds
Sesame seeds

In bowl stir together the flour, salt and 1 cup (250 mL) water. Stir until the mixture forms soft dough. Turn onto floured surface; dough will be a little sticky. Knead well for about 10 minutes until the dough is smooth. Place dough into greased bowl; cover with damp cloth. Let stand for 15 minutes.

Divide dough into 6 equal parts; roll each on a lightly floured surface into a thin rounded oblong shape, the length to fit your baking sheet. It is better that it is not even in shape. Place dough on baking sheet. Mix egg white with the 2 tbsp (25 mL) water. Brush egg mixture on dough. Sprinkle with choice of toppings, if desired. Bake in 425°F (220°C) oven for 15 minutes or until crisp and browned. Makes 6 crisp breads.

Variations:
Replace ½ cup (125 mL) of the all-purpose flour with an equal amount of one of the following: corn flour; oatmeal flour; rice flour; soya flour; or whole-wheat flour.

Baked Stuffed Mushrooms

24	mushrooms (medium to large)	24
2 tbsp	minced onion	25 mL
1	large clove garlic, minced	1
2 tsp	olive oil	10 mL
½ cup	well-drained and finely chopped cooked spinach	125 mL
¼ cup	drained small-curd skim-milk cottage cheese	50 mL
½ cup	dry bread crumbs	125 mL
½ tsp	crushed dried dill	2 mL
1 tsp	Worcestershire sauce	5 mL
Pinch	white pepper	Pinch
	Grated Parmesan cheese	

Clean mushrooms using a mushroom brush or dampened paper towel. Separate stems from caps. Mince the stems. Sauté minced stems with onion, garlic and olive oil.

Add spinach, cottage cheese, bread crumbs, dill, Worcestershire sauce and white pepper. Stir. Fill mushroom caps with spinach mixture. Sprinkle with Parmesan. (The caps can be covered in plastic wrap and refrigerated for several hours before baking. Bake just before serving.) Arrange filled caps touching in a shallow baking dish. Bake in 400°F (200°C) oven for 5 to 8 minutes just until mushrooms start to release their liquid. Transfer cooked mushrooms to warmed platter; serve at once. Makes 24 stuffed mushrooms.

Filled and Baked Giant Mushrooms

Find a quantity of very large or giant mushrooms. Break the stems off (they can be used in soups, stews or sauces). Using a dampened paper towel, wipe mushrooms. Fill mushroom caps with Salmon Filling (pg. 33), Tuna Filling (pg. 34) or Minced Chicken Filling (pg. 34). Sprinkle with grated Parmesan cheese. Broil in oven only until liquid from mushrooms just starts to appear. Time will vary depending on the size of mushrooms being used. They take little time to broil, so prepare them ahead of time and pop them into the oven a few minutes before they will be served. Serve hot or cold. (These mushrooms can be assembled as much as a day in advance and refrigerated until broiling time.)

Salmon Filling

Use this filling to stuff giant mushrooms or as a spread on crackers or bagel thins. The flavor improves if refrigerated overnight.

1	can (15½ oz/439 g) salmon	1
2 tbsp	lemon juice	25 mL
1 tsp	granulated onion	5 mL
2 tbsp	prepared white horseradish	25 mL
¼ cup	low-fat (1%) yogurt	50 mL
Pinch	white pepper	Pinch
1 tbsp	Worcestershire sauce	15 mL

Remove bones and skin from salmon; do not discard liquid. Add remaining ingredients. Mash salmon well; mixture should be thick and smooth. Makes about 1¾ cups (425 mL).

Smoked Salmon Filling
Follow the recipe for Salmon Filling. Add ⅛ tsp (0.5 mL) liquid smoke to the mixture.

Tuna Filling

Use this filling the same way as Salmon Filling.

2	cans (each 7½ oz/213 mL) water-packed low-sodium tuna	2
¼ cup	low-fat (1%) yogurt	50 mL
2 tbsp	lemon juice	25 mL
1 tbsp	Dijon mustard	15 mL
1 tsp	granulated onion	5 mL
½ tsp	ground celery seed	2 mL

Drain tuna; mash well with remaining ingredients. Makes about 1½ cups (375 mL).

Minced Chicken Filling

A good use for leftover cooked chicken. You can use turkey as well.

2 cups	cut-up cooked chicken	500 mL
⅓ cup	low-fat (1%) yogurt	75 mL
3 tbsp	light mayonnaise	50 mL
2 tbsp	Dijon mustard	25 mL
2 tsp	granulated onion	10 mL
1 tsp	ground celery seed	5 mL
¼ tsp	white pepper	1 mL

In a blender or food processor, process all ingredients until smooth but thick. Makes about 1¾ cups (425 mL).

Dried Fruit Spread (Jam)

This fruit spread is very simple, but must be kept in the refrigerator because it has no preservatives or added sugar. There is, however, natural sugar (fructose) in the fruit. Try different fruit variations including apples, apricots, peaches, pears or prunes. Use this spread as a jam. It's also great for baking.

8 oz	dried fruit	250 g

Place fruit in a small saucepan. Cover with water. Simmer until fruit is soft and most of the water is absorbed. Place in a blender or food processor; blend until smooth. A small amount of water or other liquid (see list below) may be added to adjust the consistency. Store in covered container in refrigerator. Makes about 1½ cups (375 mL).

Variations:
For a change of taste, try different combinations of liquid with the fruit. The following liquids may be substituted for the water in preparing the fruit spread: white dry wine, apple juice, orange juice, pineapple juice, diet cream soda, diet ginger ale. Use 1 tbsp (15 mL) of one of the following along with any liquid: brandy, white rum, apricot brandy, Cointreau.

Soft Whipped Diet Butter

For those of you who do not have to give up butter, this version has a lowered calorie and cholesterol count. The only thing lacking is the large list of chemical preservatives contained in the commercially prepared product. The taste is fresh and appealing. Salted butter contains about 40 mg sodium per teaspoon.

½ lb	sweet unsalted butter, at room temperature	250 g
½ cup	canola oil	125 mL
9 tbsp	skim-milk powder (not instant)	135 mL
⅓ cup	cold water	75 mL

In small mixing bowl, beat butter on low speed. While beating, add oil, skim-milk powder and water. When blended, increase mixer speed to whip for 4 to 5 minutes until butter is thick and pale in color.

Using spatula, scrape all butter into a plastic container. Refrigerate. The butter will be very spreadable from the refrigerator. Makes 1 lb (500 g).

Soft Whipped Diet Margarine
Following the directions for the Soft Whipped Diet Butter, replace sweet butter with unsalted low-cholesterol margarine.

Vegetable Pan Spray

A plastic spray bottle (1½ cups/375 mL) will be needed.

½ cup	vodka or gin	125 mL
1 tbsp	liquid lecithin	15 mL

In spray bottle, pour in vodka and lecithin. Shake before using. Great for any surface that needs to be oiled, including baking sheets, pans, muffin tins, etc. Makes ½ cup (125 mL).

Olive Oil Spray
Follow the recipe for vegetable spray, but reduce lecithin to 1½ tsp (7 mL) and add 3 tbsp (50 mL) extra virgin olive oil. Store in a plastic spray bottle. Shake before using. This olive oil spray may be used on pans, for sautéing, or any place the olive oil taste will be appropriate. For a great salad with the taste and few calories, spray the greens with olive oil spray, add some fresh ground pepper, Parmesan cheese, garlic, herb vinegar and lemon juice.

Pita or Tortilla Chips (Crackers)

These simple-to-prepare snacks can take the place of high-sodium, high-fat potato chips. They are not fried or smeared with any type of fat, bringing them in at a lower calorie count than many snacks. These are also great with spreads and dips.

	Fresh or stale pitas or tortillas	
1	egg white, beaten	1
2 tbsp	water	25 mL

Toppings:

Sesame seeds
Poppy seeds
Mixed herbs
Black pepper
Chili powder
Tarragon
Dill
Chopped onion
Granulated garlic
Granulated onion
Grated Parmesan cheese

Cut each pita open into two rounds. Mix egg white with water; brush over outside of each round. Sprinkle your choice of toppings over pitas.

Bake pitas in 400°F (200°C) oven until browned and crisp. Serve whole or broken into 3 to 4 pieces per pita round.

Variations:
• The egg-white wash may be omitted and the pita baked plain and dry. It is very good this way especially when used with dips.
• One or two pita rounds can be toasted quickly in the toaster oven for a small personal-sized snack. Try dipping in salsa or Barbecue Sauce (pg. 64).

Roasted Almonds

After making these wonderful nuts, I tried the concept with other varieties and found it to be devastatingly fantastic with any type of nut. The soy adds flavor and some salt to the nuts, but far less salt than you get in the commercially prepared nuts.

1 lb	whole unblanched, not roasted almonds	500 g
2 tbsp	low-sodium soy sauce	25 mL

Spread almonds on cookie sheet. Bake in 350°F (180°C) oven for 20 to 25 minutes until the inside of nut is toasty brown.

Pour nuts into large bowl. Immediately pour soy sauce over nuts. Mix until well coated. Spread coated nuts on cookie sheet; let dry. They can be stored in a jar for up to 2 months. Makes 1 lb (500 g).

Variations:
- Before pouring soy sauce over nuts, stir in ½ tsp (2 mL) of one of the following ingredients: granulated onion; granulated garlic; ¼ tsp (1 mL) ground ginger; ¼ tsp (1 mL) ground green peppercorns; any favorite dried herb; chili powder; or pure lemon juice.
- You can also try replacing 1 tbsp (15 mL) soy sauce with 1 tbsp (15 mL) frozen concentrated orange, lemon, pineapple or grapefruit juice (thawed). Sprinkle with ½ tsp (2 mL) pure cinnamon and mix well.
- Try this recipe with other nuts: peanuts (shelled); pumpkin seeds (raw shelled); sunflower seeds (raw shelled); cashews (raw shelled); or walnuts (raw shelled). Remember to purchase nuts that are unroasted, unblanched and not salted.

Roasted Herbed Almonds

This makes a nice change from salted roasted nuts. Food processors could learn a thing or two about great-tasting roasted nuts without salt.

1	egg white	1
1½ lb	whole unblanched, not roasted almonds	750 g
1 to 2 tbsp	dried herbs, cinnamon sugar or other spices	15 to 25 mL
	Vegetable Pan Spray (pg. 36)	

Beat egg white until frothy. Stir in almonds. Sprinkle with your favorite herbs. Toss well to distribute.

Spray cookie sheet with vegetable spray. Spread nuts over cookie sheet. Bake in 275°F (140°C) oven for 30 minutes. Shake cookie sheet and break the nuts apart. Turn off oven and let nuts remain there for 30 minutes longer until crisp and dry.

Remove nuts from oven and let cool. Store in airtight containers in refrigerator. In freezer, they will keep indefinitely. Makes 1½ lb (750 g).

Variation:
Try this recipe with other nuts, but remember to purchase unroasted and unsalted nuts.

The Soup Kettle

Basic Chicken Soup

There are many versions of this famous soup. It can be as simple as a mugful or the basis for an entire meal-in-a-bowl. When you buy chicken for soup, remember that the soup can only be as good as the quality of chicken being used. A young stewing hen is acceptable, but avoid tough fatty old birds. Leftover chicken breastbones (after deboning the breast) make a very good soup if you have enough of them. If not, freeze what you have until you have collected about 12 or more whole breast bones.

8 cups	(approx) cold water	2 L
3 lb	chicken	1.5 kg
3	carrots, cut into 2-inch (5 cm) pieces	3
3	stalks celery, cut in half	3
1	onion	1
3	cloves garlic (or 1 tbsp/ 15 mL granulated garlic)	3
2 tsp	white pepper	10 mL
3	green onions (optional)	3
2 tbsp	dried tarragon, tied into small piece of filter paper or several layers of cheesecloth	25 mL
1	slice fresh horseradish root about 1 inch (2.5 cm) thick (optional)	1
	Parsnip (optional)	
3 to 4	sprigs fresh parsley	3 to 4

In large pot, bring water to a boil.

Meanwhile, wash chicken and remove all skin and visible fat. If you are using a whole or half chicken, it is best to cut it into parts before cooking.

When water has boiled, put chicken into pot. When chicken starts to cook, stand by pot with a large spoon and container to skim off scum that will rise to top. When there is no more scum, add remaining ingredients except parsley. Simmer soup for about 1 hour over medium-low heat with the lid partially on. Add parsley. Additional water may be added to replace the liquid that will evaporate during cooking. Taste for spicing, and add extra according to your preference.

Continue to cook until chicken is soft enough to fall off the bones. Remove from heat and let soup cool for about 30 minutes.

Remove chicken meat. Remove and discard bones, horseradish root and tarragon bag. Refrigerate soup overnight to allow any fat on the surface to be removed when it is cold. The soup may be frozen, but remove the vegetables beforehand. The vegetables can be cut up and served in the soup if desired. Use boiled chicken for salads, pita fillings, or with pasta and one of the light sauces found in the chapter "All Sauced Up and Everywhere to Go." I quite often use this in my Chicken Salad (pg. 55). Makes 7 to 8 cups (1.75 to 2 L).

Variations:
Any number of additions can be made to Basic Chicken Soup to give it added flavor and zest. I usually make the basic soup and from there it is easy to create dozens of new variations. To approximately 6 cups (1.5 L) of chicken stock, try adding some of the following: 3 tbsp (50 mL) lemon juice; 1 tbsp (15 mL) Angostura Bitters; ½ cup (125 mL) chopped green onions; 3 tbsp (50 mL) low-sodium soy sauce; noodles; or rice.

Tortellini Chicken Soup
To the fat-skimmed chicken broth, add a package of frozen meat tortellini and 2 slices of fresh horseradish (optional). Cook just until tortellini is al dente. Remove horseradish; discard. Serve soup hot with a sprinkling of Parmesan cheese.

Italian Stracciatella

3	egg whites	3
2 tbsp	water	25 mL
2 tbsp	all-purpose flour	25 mL
2 tbsp	grated Parmesan cheese	25 mL
	Freshly ground black pepper	
5 to 6 cups	(approx) chicken stock	1.25 L
	Grated Parmesan cheese	

Whisk together egg whites, water, flour, cheese and pepper. Bring chicken stock to a boil. Using a measuring cup with a spout, very slowly pour a small stream of egg mixture into boiling soup, stirring with wire whisk. Cook on medium heat for 5 minutes. The egg mixture will form floating strands. Serve hot with a sprinkling of Parmesan cheese. Makes 6 cups (1.5 L).

Chicken-Soup Ice-Cubes

Reserve a quantity of fat-skimmed chicken soup to fill several ice-cube trays; freeze. When frozen, remove the cubes from the trays and place in a plastic bag. These cubes are handy for a quick cup of soup or for use in many recipes. The cubes are also convenient for use in making gravy or as a poaching liquid. When a family member comes home sick with a cold or the flu, an instant hot mug of homemade chicken soup will be at hand.

Note:
If you don't have chicken soup cubes on hand, a good alternative is low-sodium chicken soup powder. The powder may also be used along with the cubes to intensify the homemade soup flavor. Beef soup ice-cubes and low-sodium beef soup powder may be used in the same way.

Leek and Lemon Soup

2 lb	leeks (white part only), trimmed	1 kg
1 tbsp	virgin olive oil	15 mL
1	lemon	1
1 cup	finely chopped celery	250 mL
Half	pkg (10 oz/284 g) frozen chopped spinach, thawed, or 1 cup (250 mL) fresh spinach	Half
4 cups	chicken stock made from salt-free chicken soup powder	1 L
	White pepper	
¼ cup	fresh minced parsley	50 mL

Chop leeks coarsely. In deep soup pot, sauté leeks and olive oil with the strained juice of the lemon. Cover and simmer on medium-low heat for 10 minutes. Add celery; cook for 10 minutes. Add spinach; cook for 2 minutes. Add the chicken stock, pepper and parsley. Simmer for 10 minutes. Serve hot. Makes 6 servings.

Creating Your Own Soup-mix Base

Soup bases can be used to create many varieties of soups just by adding whatever is available in your refrigerator.

Split Pea Soup Mix

More than one batch can be made but make up each one
separately.

¼ cup	quick-cooking barley	50 mL
¼ cup	yellow split peas	50 mL
¼ cup	green split peas	50 mL
1 tbsp	granulated onion	15 mL
1 tbsp	granulated garlic	15 mL
1 tbsp	chili powder	15 mL
2 tbsp	Season All	25 mL
1 tsp	powdered sage (or 2 tsp/ 10 mL dried sage)	5 mL
¼ cup	salt-free chicken soup powder	50 mL
1 tbsp	dried tarragon	15 mL

Mix together all ingredients and store in covered container or
plastic bag. Makes 1 batch.

Vegetable Soup Mix

¼ cup	quick-cooking barley	50 mL
¼ cup	lima beans or small white beans	50 mL
¼ cup	green or yellow split peas	50 mL
1 tbsp	granulated onion	15 mL
¼ cup	dried mushrooms	50 mL
2 tbsp	Season All	25 mL
1½ tsp	granulated garlic	7 mL
¼ cup	dehydrated vegetables	50 mL
1 tbsp	chili powder	15 mL
¼ cup	salt-free chicken soup powder	50 mL

Mix together all ingredients and store in covered container or
plastic bag. Makes 1 batch.

Basic Cooking Directions for Soup Mixes
In large pot, boil 8 cups (2 L) water. Add 1 batch soup mix.
Bring liquid back to boil; cover and lower heat so soup will
gently cook for 1 hour.

Add 1½ cups (375 mL) raw thinly sliced carrots if desired.
Cook for about 10 minutes. Add any variety of other softer
types of vegetables. Cook 5–8 minutes. Season to taste.

If desired, near the end of the cooking time for Split Pea or
Vegetable Soup, chopped leftover chicken, turkey, roast beef
or cooked extra-lean ground meat of any type may be added
to make a hearty soup. Makes 8 cups (2 L).

Italian Vegetable Soup

The variety of vegetables in this soup can include whatever
you have available, so change them around from time to time.

8 cups	water	2 L
3	tomatoes (can be overripe), chopped	3
1	onion, chopped	1
4	cloves garlic, minced (or 1 tbsp/15 mL granulated garlic)	4
2	carrots, chopped	2
3 tbsp	low-sodium chicken soup powder	50 mL
2	stalks celery, chopped	2
12	green beans, cut in ½-inch (1 cm) pieces	12
1	potato, peeled and diced	1
3 oz	tomato paste	75 mL
1 tbsp	tarragon	15 mL
1 tbsp	basil	15 mL
1 tbsp	oregano	15 mL

1 tbsp	thyme	15 mL
2 tbsp	chili powder	25 mL
1 tsp	freshly ground black pepper	5 mL
¼ cup	small-shape pasta	50 mL
Half	pkg (10 oz/284 g) frozen chopped spinach	Half
6	mushrooms, sliced	6
2 tbsp	all-purpose flour (optional)	25 mL
¼ cup	water (optional)	50 mL
1 tbsp	extra virgin olive oil	15 mL
	Grated Parmesan cheese	

In large pot, boil water. Add tomatoes, onion, garlic, carrots and soup powder. Cook, partially covered, for 20 minutes. (It may be necessary to add 1 cup/250 mL water because of evaporation.)

Add celery, green beans, potato, tomato paste, tarragon, basil, oregano, thyme, chili powder and pepper. Cook for 15 minutes. Add pasta, spinach and mushrooms. If you wish to thicken the broth, in a measuring cup dissolve flour in ¼ cup (50 mL) water; stir into soup. Cook for 10 minutes. Add olive oil. Season to taste. Serve with a sprinkling of Parmesan cheese. Makes approximately 8 cups (2 L).

Variations:
A soup bone with some meat on it may be added at the beginning, when the water comes to a boil and before the vegetables are added. Skim the scum from the surface that will form as the soup bone starts to cook.

Basic Beef Stock

Basic beef (or veal) stock can be made from any cuts of meat, and a bone will greatly enhance the quality and flavor. This soup stock can become the base for many varieties of soup. Some soup stock should be reserved, after skimming all the fat, and frozen in ice-cube trays, as is suggested with the chicken soup stock. The uses for frozen beef stock cubes are almost limitless.

9 cups	water	2.25 L
2 or 3	bones with meat clinging	2 or 3
3/4 lb	(approx) stewing beef or other cuts	375 g
3	carrots, cut in 2-inch (5 cm) pieces	3
3	stalks celery, cut in half	3
1	onion	1
3	cloves garlic, minced	3
1½ tsp	ground black pepper	7 mL
1 tbsp	Season All	15 mL
2 tbsp	dry mustard	25 mL
3 tbsp	Worcestershire sauce	50 mL

In large pot, bring water to a boil. Add meat bones and stewing beef. When meat starts to cook, a scum will rise to surface; skim this off. Add carrots, celery, onion, garlic, pepper, Season All, mustard and Worcestershire sauce.

Cook, partially covered, for 1½ hours over medium-low heat until meat is very tender. Season to taste. Let cool. Remove all bones, meat and vegetables when the soup has cooled. Refrigerate until cold; skim any fat from the top. Makes 8 cups (2 L) liquid.

Variations:
Use fat-skimmed stock for other soups; freeze a quantity in ice-cube trays. The meat can be used in the soup or in other recipes.

Japanese Beef and Mushroom Soup
To 4 cups (1 L) beef stock, add 1 cup (250 mL) sliced mushrooms and 2 tbsp (25 mL) chopped green onions; cook over medium heat for 2 to 3 minutes. Mushrooms should still be crisp. Add 2 tbsp (25 mL) low-sodium soy sauce.

Onion Soup

I have two methods for making this soup; one requires
making a beef stock, the other is so fast I call it my Almost
Instant Onion Soup. Both taste great.

2	onions (cooking or Spanish)	2
2	cloves garlic, minced	2
2 tbsp	Scotch	25 mL
4 cups	beef stock or 4 cups (1 L) water with ¼ cup (50 mL) low-sodium beef soup base	1 L
½ tsp	fresh ground pepper	2 mL
1½ tsp	caraway seeds, tied in cheesecloth (optional)	7 mL
¼ cup	grated Parmesan cheese	50 mL

Slice onions in half from top to bottom. Slice the halves into
¼-inch (5 mm) slices. Preheat a skillet, spray with vegetable
spray. In the skillet, sauté onions and garlic until translucent
and lightly browned. Add the Scotch; cook for 1 minute.

Transfer onions to large pot; pour in beef stock. Add
pepper and bag of caraway seeds (if using). Simmer, covered,
over low heat for 10 minutes. Remove and discard caraway
seeds.

Serve with a sprinkling of Parmesan. Makes 4 servings.

Variations:
• A combination of beef stock and chicken stock may be used
for a slightly different flavor.
• To make Onion Mushroom Soup, in the last 2 or 3 minutes
of cooking, add about 1 cup (250 mL) sliced fresh
mushrooms.

Hearty Beef and Barley Soup

This is a great soup for a cold winter day — it can become a whole meal-in-a-bowl with the addition of hot fresh rolls, biscuits or homemade bread. It can be made thick (almost like a stew) or thin, depending on your own tastes.

6 cups	water	1.5 L
1½ lb	(approx) any type of lean beef (stewing beef, round, etc.), cut in 1-inch (2.5 cm) pieces	750 g
½ cup	pearl barley	125 mL
½ cup	baby lima beans	125 mL
1	onion, chopped finely	1
3	large carrots, peeled and cut in ¼-inch (5 mm) slices	3
1 tbsp	granulated garlic	15 mL
1 tbsp	granulated onion	15 mL
1 tsp	sage	5 mL
1½ tsp	freshly ground pepper	7 mL
4 tsp	Season All	20 mL
½ cup	frozen green peas	125 mL
1 cup	thickly sliced mushrooms	250 mL
3 tbsp	all-purpose flour (optional)	50 mL
1 cup	cold water (optional)	250 mL

In large soup pot, bring water to a boil; add beef. Cook meat over medium-high heat, skimming the scum that rises to the surface. Once the scum no longer appears, add barley and baby lima beans. Cook, partially covered, over medium heat for 45 minutes. Add chopped onion, carrots, garlic, granulated onion, sage, pepper and Season All; simmer for 30 minutes. Check the level of the broth — some of it will have evaporated during cooking; add water if desired. Stir in green peas and mushrooms; simmer for 20 minutes.

If you want to thicken the broth, dissolve flour in 1 cup (250 mL) cold water; add to the cooking soup. Season to taste.

Refrigerate the soup overnight and skim off any fat before using. Makes 6 cups (1.5 L).

Golden Carrot Soup

This is a great-looking hot carrot soup. It packs a lot of nutrition, but this version is calorie- and fat-reduced.

4	carrots, diced	4
2	potatoes, peeled and chopped	2
2	stalks celery, chopped	2
1	onion, chopped	1
3 cups	chicken stock or water mixed with 3 tbsp (50 mL) salt-free chicken soup base	750 mL
4 tsp	tarragon	20 mL
⅓ cup	instant skim-milk powder	75 mL
1 cup	cold water	250 mL
1 tbsp	extra virgin olive oil	15 mL

In covered pot, boil carrots, potatoes, celery, onion, chicken stock and tarragon until vegetables are tender.

Let cool; purée in a blender or food processor.

Return purée to the pot. Dissolve skim-milk powder in water; slowly mix in with purée. Reheat gently over low heat; add olive oil. Makes 4 cups (1 L).

Basic Fish Stock

This is essential for making good fish soup, and is made from the scrap parts of the fish.

6 cups	water	1.5 L
2 lb	bones, heads and tails of sole, halibut, salmon, or other fish, well washed	1 kg
2	carrots, cut in 2-inch (5 cm) pieces	2
1	large leek, chopped	1
2 to 3	stalks celery, chopped	2 to 3
1/2	bunch fresh parsley, chopped	1/2
3 tbsp	lemon juice	50 mL
1/4 tsp	white pepper	1 mL
1 tbsp	tarragon	15 mL
1 1/2 tsp	granulated garlic	7 mL
1 1/2 tsp	granulated onion	7 mL

In large pot, bring all ingredients slowly to a boil. Reduce heat; simmer, partially covered, for 1 hour. The broth will need to be skimmed from time to time, using a large spoon to remove the scum that will rise to the top. Strain the stock. Use immediately or refrigerate for up to 3 days. The stock without the vegetables may be frozen for several months. Makes 5 cups (1.25 L).

Using Fish Stock
Freeze a quantity of the stock in ice-cube trays. Bag when frozen and use as liquid when steaming fish, for a quick cup of fish soup, or as the base for light sauces for fish. Fast and light fish sauces for pasta can be made with these cubes.

Fish Chowder

This basic chowder can be made with any type of fish; variety will add flavor to the chowder. A firm-flesh fish will be better suited to long cooking times. When using a more delicate fish, start with a fish stock and reduce the cooking time so the fish will not fall apart in the soup.

2	large carrots, thinly sliced	2
2	stalks celery, diced	2
1	onion, diced	1
1 tbsp	virgin olive oil	15 mL
4 cups	water	1 L
½ lb	firm-flesh fish (thick), cut in chunks	250 g
2 cups	diced potatoes	500 mL
¼ tsp	white pepper	1 mL
1½ tsp	granulated garlic	7 mL
¼ cup	dry white wine	50 mL
1 cup	instant skim-milk powder	250 mL
3 tbsp	all-purpose flour	50 mL
1 cup	skim milk	250 mL

In skillet, sauté carrots, celery and onion in olive oil until onion is translucent.

In separate, large pot, bring water to a boil. Add fish.

Return water to a boil; skim the water. Add potatoes and sautéed vegetables. Cook over low heat for 5 minutes. Add pepper, garlic and wine. Cook for 10 minutes. Combine skim-milk powder with flour; dissolve in skim milk. Slowly add to soup.

Simmer over low heat for 5 minutes to thicken. Makes 5 to 6 servings.

Salmon Bisque

Very easy to make, this bisque is a nice change from chowder.
Garnish with a sprig of parsley if you like.

1	onion, finely chopped	1
1	stalk celery, finely chopped	1
3½ cups	skim milk	875 mL
1 cup	instant skim-milk powder	250 mL
3 tbsp	all-purpose flour	50 mL
1	can (7½ oz/213 mL) salmon, drained, skin and bones removed	1
¼ tsp	white pepper	1 mL
1½ tsp	tarragon, crushed	7 mL
¼ cup	dry white wine	50 mL

In saucepan sprayed with vegetable spray, sauté onion and
celery.

Meanwhile, in bowl, mix skim milk with skim-milk
powder; set aside.

Add flour to sautéed vegetables; stir well. Slowly add milk;
cook to make a roux, stirring constantly. Add salmon,
pepper, tarragon and wine; cook and stir over low heat until
creamy and smooth. Remove from heat and let cool.

Pour soup into blender; process until smooth. Reheat
gently before serving. Makes 4 servings.

Variations:
• Substitute water-packed tuna for the salmon.
• Substitute cooked shrimp for the salmon. A small amount of
  small shrimps or chopped large cooked shrimps may be
  added to the bisque when heating to serve.
• Substitute cooked lobster meat for the salmon. A small
  amount of chopped lobster meat may be added to the bisque
  when heating to serve.

Dressing Up a Salad

Salad Dressings:
Fighting the Invisible Calories

Most commercially available dressings, with the exception of a few produced for calorie-restricted diets, contain a large portion of oil. Most typical dressings contain 70 to 80 calories per tablespoon (15 mL). Sodium in that same tablespoon can range from 115 mg to 400 mg. Sugar can also vary, from 1/4 tsp (1 mL) per tablespoon (15 mL) of dressing to more than 1/2 tsp (2 mL). This is one of the great sources of invisible calories from fat that many of us consume while eating what we might think of as a diet meal. Great-tasting, low-calorie dressings can be easily prepared at home with minimal time and effort.

Create a Salad

The best salads are made from whatever happens to be available — leftover cooked cold vegetables; leftover lean meats, chicken or fish; and chopped raw vegetables. Cheeses (low-fat and low-sodium) of all types (used sparingly), and low-fat (1%) cottage cheese mixed into the salad add flavor and protein.

If the salad is to be the main course of the meal, make sure that some form of protein (meat, fish, chicken, cheese) is included. Raw vegetables should be cut into small or bite-sized pieces. Some vegetables, like carrots and zucchini, can be sliced thinly or shredded.

Salad can be washed and cut up hours before serving. Cover it in a bowl, or store the salad in a closed plastic bag in the refrigerator until ready to use.

Dressing should be added just before serving (when the salad has lettuce) unless the salad is a marinated type. Marinated salads usually need to develop flavor for a minimum period; overnight is usually best.

Great Garlic Dressing

1 cup	low-fat (1%) cottage cheese	250 mL
2	cloves garlic	2
1 tsp	freshly ground black pepper	5 mL
1 tbsp	extra virgin olive oil	15 mL
3 tbsp	dry white wine	50 mL
3 to 4 tbsp	skim milk	50 mL

In blender or food processor, purée all ingredients. Refrigerate for several hours before using. The flavor will improve when it is allowed to stand overnight. Leftovers will keep for up to 1 week if the cheese is fresh. Makes 1 cup (250 mL).

Chicken Salad

This is a wonderful way to use up leftover chicken after making chicken soup. Any kind of leftover chicken or turkey can be used. My family really enjoys this for a light dinner in the summer. A baked fruit dessert goes well after this salad.

2 cups	(approx) chicken, turkey or roast beef, cut up	500 mL
1	head lettuce, torn in bite-sized pieces	1

Dressing:

2 tbsp	virgin olive oil	25 mL
2 tbsp	cornstarch	25 mL
1 cup	low-fat milk	250 mL
2 tsp	granulated onion	10 mL
¼ tsp	white pepper	1 mL
½ tsp	granulated garlic	2 mL
2 tbsp	light mayonnaise	25 mL
4 tbsp	grated Parmesan cheese	50 mL
	Freshly ground white pepper	

In saucepan over medium heat, heat and blend olive oil and cornstarch to make a paste. Slowly add milk, stirring until all

milk is added. Heat until thick. Remove from heat; mix in
onion, pepper and garlic. Let sauce cool in refrigerator, about
1 hour. Stir in mayonnaise.

Store cut-up meat, lettuce and dressing in refrigerator until
just before ready to serve. In large salad bowl, mix meat and
dressing into lettuce. Continue to mix and toss until the
dressing is well distributed. Sprinkle with Parmesan and
pepper to taste. Makes 4 to 5 servings.

Blue Cheese Dressing

The amount of blue cheese used in this recipe is very small,
but being a very pungent cheese, the flavor is sensational
when allowed to develop. Excess blue cheese is not needed
for this recipe; the leftover blue cheese can be frozen for use
in another batch of dressing.

2 oz	blue cheese, crumbled	50 g
1 cup	skim-milk yogurt	250 mL
½ cup	low-fat (1%) cottage cheese	125 mL
3 tbsp	dry white wine	50 mL
½ tsp	granulated onion	2 mL

In small bowl, place blue cheese, yogurt, cottage cheese, wine
and onion. Using spoon, mix until well blended.

Store dressing in covered container in refrigerator for
several hours before using to let flavor develop.

This will produce a chunky dressing. If a smoother
dressing is wanted, place dressing in a blender; purée until
smooth. Makes 1½ cups (375 mL).

Spinach Salad with Warm Mustard Dressing

2	bunches fresh spinach, torn in bite-sized pieces	2
2 tbsp	extra virgin olive oil	25 mL
2 tbsp	cornstarch	25 mL
1 cup	skim milk	250 mL
¼ tsp	white pepper	1 mL
1 tsp	granulated garlic	5 mL
1 tbsp	tarragon	15 mL
2 tbsp	Dijon mustard	25 mL
2 tbsp	light mayonnaise	25 mL
	Grated Parmesan cheese	

Wash and dry spinach. Place in large bowl. Refrigerate.

In saucepan over medium heat, heat and blend olive oil and cornstarch to make a paste. Slowly add milk while stirring. Cook until thick. Remove from heat; add pepper, garlic and tarragon. Let dressing cool for 10 minutes. In separate bowl, mix mustard into mayonnaise. Add mustard mayonnaise to dressing, stirring to blend. Just before serving, pour warm dressing over spinach. Sprinkle with Parmesan cheese. Makes 5 to 6 servings.

Caesar Salad with Dressing #1

1	large head romaine lettuce, torn into bite-sized pieces	1

Dressing:

4 oz	light cream cheese	125 g
⅓ cup	skim milk	75 mL
1 tbsp	extra virgin olive oil	15 mL
1 tbsp	chopped fresh garlic (or 1½ tsp/7 mL) granulated garlic)	15 mL
2 tsp	granulated onion	10 mL
3 tbsp	lemon juice	50 mL
1½ tsp	freshly ground black pepper	7 mL
¼ cup	grated Parmesan cheese	50 mL

Wash and dry lettuce; place in large salad bowl. Refrigerate.

In blender, purée cream cheese, milk, oil, garlic, onion, lemon juice, pepper and half of the Parmesan until smooth. Season to taste. Spoon out enough of the dressing to coat romaine lettuce well. Sprinkle remaining Parmesan over salad. Makes 5 to 6 servings. Refrigerate leftover dressing.

Note:
When adding and tossing any dressing into a salad, go lightly on the amount of dressing that is being added. A lot of tossing and mixing will distribute a small amount well; this will reduce the calories and fat. Too much dressing will also cause the lettuce to wilt faster. It is better to toss small amounts of any dressing through the salad than let it be added by each person at the table.

Caesar Salad with Dressing #2

1	large head romaine lettuce, torn in bite-sized pieces	1

Dressing:

1 cup	low-fat (1%) cottage cheese, puréed in blender or food processor	250 mL
1 tbsp	extra virgin olive oil	15 mL
1 tsp	Worcestershire sauce	5 mL
3 tbsp	dry white wine	50 mL
1½ tsp	granulated garlic	7 mL
1 tbsp	Dijon mustard	15 mL
2 tbsp	lemon juice	25 mL
2 tsp	freshly ground black pepper	10 mL
¼ cup	grated Parmesan cheese	50 mL

Wash and dry lettuce; place in large salad bowl. Refrigerate.

In 2-cup (500 mL) measure, mix together all dressing ingredients. Pour over lettuce; toss well just before serving.

Makes 5 to 6 servings.

Note:
Extra freshly ground pepper may be added at the table.

Lime and Tarragon Dressing

¼ cup	lime juice	50 mL
2 tbsp	extra virgin olive oil	25 mL
1 tsp	tarragon	5 mL
3 tbsp	dry white wine	50 mL
½ tsp	freshly ground green peppercorns	2 mL

In 2-cup (500 mL) measure, mix together all ingredients.
Makes ½ cup (125 mL).

Tomato Slices with Herbs and Parmesan

Easy and fast to prepare, this dish can accompany other
vegetables for dinner or lunch. It can also be an appetizer, and
with the addition of protein it can become a light meal itself.

Tomatoes
Granulated garlic
Italian herbs (blend of
   thyme, rosemary and
   oregano)
Grated Parmesan cheese
Extra virgin olive oil
   (optional)

Wash as many tomatoes as are needed (allow 2 to 3 slices per
person as a side dish or appetizer); slice tomatoes ¼-inch (5
mm) thick. Place tomato slices on large platter (slices may
touch but not overlap). Sprinkle over each slice, according to
taste, garlic, herbs and cheese. Drizzle olive oil over tomatoes,
if using. (Olive oil is optional if calories are being counted.)
Serve cold or at room temperature.

Variations:
Any of your favorite spices and herbs (dried or fresh) can be used.

Cut the slices a bit thicker, about ½ inch (1 cm). Place the slices on a heatproof platter or microwave-safe dish. Top each slice with a thin slice of skim-milk mozzarella cheese or 1 tbsp (15 mL) shredded mozzarella. Other cheeses that melt easily will work well. Broil the tomatoes until the cheese has melted or cook in the microwave just to melt the cheese. Try a coating of prepared or Dijon mustard on the tomato with a thin slice of low-fat cheddar melted on top.

You can eat this hot or cold. Other possibilities for creating your own: fresh or dried dill; low-fat (1%) cottage cheese; fresh or dried chives; yogurt sprinkled with dill, chives or parsley; granulated onion; freshly ground pepper; chili powder; fresh or dried parsley.

Potato Salad

This method of making potato salad can vary depending on the other vegetables used besides potato. The main point here is a good-tasting potato salad with a fraction of the fat and calories.

2 tbsp	virgin olive oil	25 mL
2 tbsp	cornstarch	25 mL
1 cup	low-fat milk	250 mL
1 tbsp	granulated sugar	15 mL
1 tsp	ground celery seed	5 mL
1 tsp	dry mustard	5 mL
1 tbsp	granulated onion	15 mL
¼ cup	chopped green onion	50 mL
¼ tsp	white pepper	1 mL
1 tbsp	low-sodium tomato soup powder or 1 tbsp (15 mL) tomato paste	15 mL

1 tbsp	tarragon	15 mL
¼ cup	light mayonnaise	50 mL
8	large potatoes, cooked in jackets and cooled	8

In saucepan over medium heat, blend olive oil and cornstarch to make a paste. Slowly add milk, stirring until all milk is added. Stir in sugar, cooking until thick. Add celery seed, mustard, granulated onion, green onion, white pepper, tomato soup and tarragon. Heat until mixture begins to bubble; remove from heat. Cool sauce in refrigerator for about 1 hour. Add mayonnaise; stir well.

Peel potatoes; cut into bite-sized pieces. Place potatoes in large bowl; toss with mayonnaise mixture. Let salad stand for at least 1 hour in refrigerator before serving. Makes 10 to 12 servings.

Variation:
Before tossing with the dressing, add any of the following chopped raw vegetables with the potatoes: 3 stalks of celery, finely chopped; half of a blanched and peeled sweet red or green pepper, finely chopped; 2 large raw carrots, grated.

Create a Dressing
Any type of low-calorie dressing can be quickly made by using a base of low-fat (1%) cottage cheese and a blender or food processor. With this base, try the following combinations.

French Dressing

1 cup	low-fat (1%) cottage cheese	250 mL
4 tsp	low-salt tomato soup powder or 2 tbsp (25 mL) tomato paste	20 mL
2 tbsp	dry white wine	25 mL
2 tbsp	extra virgin olive oil	25 mL
2 tsp	granulated onion	10 mL
1/2 tsp	white pepper	2 mL

In food processor, add all ingredients; process until smooth.
Makes 1¼ cups (300 mL).

Creamy Parsley Dressing

1 cup	low-fat (1%) cottage cheese	250 mL
1/2 cup	chopped fresh parsley (stems removed)	125 mL
2 tsp	granulated onion	10 mL
1 tsp	freshly ground green peppercorns	5 mL
1/4 cup	grated Parmesan cheese	50 mL
3 tbsp	dry white wine	50 mL
2 tbsp	extra virgin olive oil	25 mL

In food processor, add all ingredients; process until smooth.
Makes 2 cups (500 mL).

Tuna Cottage Salad

This a nice change from tuna salad. It can be used for a sandwich, in a pita with shredded lettuce, or scooped onto a lettuce leaf. It makes a light and easy dinner on a hot summer night.

½ cup	low-fat (1%) cottage cheese	125 mL
1	can (7½ oz/213 mL) water-packed low-sodium tuna	1
1 tsp	pure lemon juice	5 mL
1 tbsp	chopped green onion or parsley	15 mL
½ tsp	granulated onion	2 mL
2 tbsp	(approx) light mayonnaise	25 mL

In blender or food processor, process cottage cheese until smooth. Drain water from the tuna; mash tuna well in a bowl. Add cottage cheese; mix. Add remaining ingredients, mixing well after each addition. (The mayonnaise should be added 1 tbsp/15 mL at a time to obtain the correct texture.) Makes about 1½ cups (375 mL).

Variation:
When serving on a lettuce leaf or in a pita pocket, sprinkle grated carrots, alfalfa sprouts or a combination of both over the tuna salad.

All Sauced Up and Everywhere to Go

Barbecue Sauce

My children claim this sauce is great on everything. I usually keep some prepared sauce on hand, ready for anything. This version contains far less sugar than most commercially prepared barbecue sauces.

For the base of this sauce you can use prepared ketchup or sodium- and sugar-reduced prepared ketchup. If you want something with absolutely no sugar or salt, pure tomato paste works well. (See Diet Barbecue Sauce, pg. 65.) The hickory-smoked version is great, too. The quantity may be doubled.

1 cup	ketchup	250 mL
2 tbsp	Worcestershire sauce	25 mL
3 tbsp	prepared mustard	50 mL
1 tsp	granulated onion	5 mL
1 tsp	granulated garlic	5 mL
1 to 2 tbsp	(more if you like it very spicy) chili powder	15 to 25 mL
1 to 2 tsp	(for spicy sauce) hot pepper sauce, or 1 tbsp (15 mL) (for suicide sauce)	5 to 10 mL

In bowl, mix together all ingredients. Season to taste. Store in covered container in refrigerator. Use sauce with any meat, poultry or fish. Makes 1 cup (250 mL).

Variation:
For hickory flavor, add ¼ tsp (1 mL) liquid hickory smoke.

Diet Barbecue Sauce

1	can (5½ oz/156 mL) tomato paste	1
½ cup	water	125 mL
2 tbsp	dry white wine	25 mL
2 tbsp	Worcestershire sauce	25 mL
3 tbsp	prepared mustard	50 mL
1 tbsp	granulated garlic	15 mL
1 tbsp	granulated onion	15 mL
1 to 2 tbsp	chili powder	15 to 25 mL
1 to 2 tsp	(for spicy sauce) hot pepper sauce, or 1 tbsp (15 mL) (for suicide sauce)	5 to 10 mL
	Artificial sweetener	

In bowl, mix together all ingredients except artificial sweetener. Season with artificial sweetener to taste. Store in covered container in refrigerator. Makes 1 cup (250 mL).

Chinese Marinade or Cooking Sauce

This very tasty sauce can be used in a variety of ways, and some recipes in other chapters use this sauce. But try it with some of your own favorites. Good with beef, veal, poultry or fish.

½ cup	finely chopped green onions	125 mL
3 tbsp	low-sodium soy sauce	50 mL
3 tbsp	dry white wine	50 mL
½ tsp	ground ginger (more if you like it stronger)	2 mL
1 tbsp	sesame seed oil	15 mL
½ cup	water	125 mL

In measuring cup, mix together all ingredients. This sauce can be used as a marinade or as a cooking liquid.

Make ahead and store in refrigerator. Makes ¾ cup (175 mL).

Variations:
• Thicken sauce by adding 1 to 2 tbsp (15 mL to 25 mL) cornstarch to the water; cook sauce until it becomes thick and translucent.
• Instead of water, any type of stock may be substituted: chicken, beef, veal or fish. Low-sodium chicken or beef soup powder may be dissolved in the water.

Mustard Tarragon Sauce

This is wonderful brushed on fish for broiling. Also good with chicken and turkey.

1 tbsp	light mayonnaise	15 mL
⅓ cup	skim-milk yogurt	75 mL
2 tbsp	Dijon mustard	25 mL
1 tsp	lemon juice	5 mL
1 tsp	crushed tarragon	5 mL

In small container, mix together all ingredients. Let sauce stand for 2 hours at room temperature before using, to let flavor develop. Store in refrigerator. Makes ½ cup (125 mL).

Basic Fast Pasta Sauce

This sauce can be served with any shape or type of pasta. It is great for stewing chicken or fish.

1	onion, chopped	1
1	can (28 oz/796 mL) stewed tomatoes (no salt or sugar added), chopped	1
1	can (5½ oz/156 mL) tomato paste (no sugar or salt)	1
1 cup	water	250 mL
½ cup	dry white wine or water	125 mL
1 tbsp	granulated garlic	15 mL

½ tsp	white pepper	2 mL
1 tbsp	chili powder	15 mL
2 tbsp	mixed Italian herbs	25 mL
1 tsp	tarragon	5 mL
1 tbsp	parsley	15 mL
1 tbsp	extra virgin olive oil	15 mL

In dry non-stick skillet, sauté onions until soft and slightly brown. Transfer onions to large pot. Add tomatoes, tomato paste, water and wine. Stir well. Bring sauce to a simmer; add remaining ingredients except olive oil. Simmer sauce gently for 10 minutes, with pot partially covered. Adjust spices for personal taste. (This sauce can also be adjusted for desired thickness. Add water to thin, or use 2 tbsp/25 mL flour mixed with ¼ cup/50 mL water to thicken.) When cooking is done, add olive oil. Makes 3½ cups (875 mL).

Variations:
• Add ¼ to ½ lb (125 g to 250 g) small whole or sliced fresh mushrooms near the end of the cooking time.
• Meat Sauce: Add to the finished sauce 1 lb (500 g) any type of extra-lean ground meat browned in a non-stick pan. Season to taste.
• Add raw shrimp, scallops or chunks of any firm-flesh fish 5 minutes before the sauce is finished.
• In addition to or instead of meats, add vegetables and cooked beans to this sauce. Leftover cooked vegetables should be added only at the end; hard or raw types should be cooked before adding; softer types can be simmered in the sauce for about 5 minutes. Try carrots, broccoli, peas, green beans, snow peas, asparagus, spinach.

Teriyaki Sauce

The teriyaki sauce available in stores, though it tastes fine, contains a large amount of sugar and salt. This healthier sauce can be prepared easily at home. Use as a marinade for fish, poultry or meat. It makes a great dipping sauce, too.

½ cup	low-sodium soy sauce	125 mL
½ cup	Japanese rice wine or dry white wine	125 mL
1½ tsp	rice vinegar	7 mL
1½ tsp	brown sugar	7 mL
1 tsp	ground ginger	5 mL
½ tsp	granulated garlic	2 mL
1 tbsp	cornstarch (optional)	15 mL

In 2-cup (500 mL) measure, mix all ingredients except cornstarch. Let stand, covered, for about 2 hours to let flavors develop.

To thicken for brushing onto meats, fish or poultry, add cornstarch; heat to thicken. Store leftovers in a sealed jar. Makes 1 cup (250 mL).

Sesame Lemon Marinade

This marinade can be poured over meat, poultry or fish.

½ cup	low-sodium soy sauce	125 mL
½ cup	lemon juice	125 mL
1 tsp	sesame seed oil	5 mL
1 tsp	ground ginger	5 mL

In bowl, combine all ingredients. Refrigerate to let flavors develop. Makes 1 cup (250 mL).

Spicy Sesame Marinade

Use this marinade poured over meat, poultry or fish.

¼ cup	low-sodium soy sauce	50 mL
¼ cup	dry white wine	50 mL
1 tbsp	sesame seed oil	15 mL
1 tsp	tarragon	5 mL
1 tsp	dry mustard	5 mL

In bowl, combine all ingredients. Refrigerate 2 hours to let flavors develop. Makes ½ cup (125 mL).

Basic White Sauce

Basic white sauce can be made from the lowest calorie- and fat-sparing ingredients. Once the sauce is made, endless types of herbs, spices and other ingredients can be added to flavor this simple sauce.

Be aware that the additions, if not controlled, can add enormous amounts of fats, sodium and calories.

2 tbsp	margarine or canola oil (olive oil may be substituted if appropriate to the use of the sauce)	25 mL
2 tbsp	all-purpose flour	25 mL
1 cup	skim milk (if a richer sauce is required, add ¼ cup/ 50 mL of instant skim-milk powder to liquid milk)	250 mL

In small saucepan over medium heat, melt margarine. Mix in flour, stirring until blended. Add 3 tbsp (50 mL) of the milk. As soon as it is mixed in, add another 3 tbsp (50 mL) of the milk. Gradually add remaining milk while stirring. Remove from heat when sauce is thick and bubbling. Makes 1 cup (250 mL).

Variation:
Add 2 to 3 tbsp (25 mL to 50 mL) of strong, flavorful low-fat cheese to create a cheese sauce sparing on the calories and cholesterol.

Cranberry Sauce

2 cups	fresh or frozen cranberries	500 mL
2½ cups	water	625 mL
¼ cup	brown sugar or brown sugar substitute	50 mL
¼ cup	frozen concentrated unsweetened orange juice	50 mL
¼ cup	cornstarch	50 mL
⅓ cup	water	75 mL
2 tbsp	white rum	25 mL

In large pot, cook cranberries with 2½ cups (625 mL) water, brown sugar and orange juice. In separate bowl, whisk together cornstarch and ⅓ cup (75 mL) water. When berries pop open, stir in cornstarch mixture. Stir in white rum. Cook until thickened. Pour into a covered container; chill. Makes 3½ cups (875 mL).

Variations:
Substitute 2½ cups (625 mL) unsweetened pineapple juice for same amount of water. Omit brown sugar. Mix in 1 tsp (5 mL) cinnamon, if desired.

Cranberry Apple Sauce
Just after the berries pop open, add 2 large grated unpeeled apples. Cook for another 2 to 3 minutes. Remove from heat; mix in 1 tsp (5 mL) cinnamon.

Light Tarragon and Basil Pasta Sauce

Pour this sauce over any pasta. Fish, seafood or chicken can
be added with delicious results.

2½ cups	water	625 mL
2 tbsp	low-sodium tomato soup mix	25 mL
2 tbsp	red vermouth or dry red wine	25 mL
3 tbsp	all-purpose flour	50 mL
1 cup	water	250 mL
2 tsp	granulated garlic	10 mL
2 tsp	basil	10 mL
2 tsp	tarragon	10 mL
¼ tsp	white pepper	1 mL
2 tbsp	extra virgin olive oil	25 mL

In saucepan, heat 2½ cups (625 mL) water; add soup mix and
vermouth. Dissolve flour in 1 cup (250 mL) water. Stir into
heated mixture; cook, stirring, until thickened. Add garlic,
basil, tarragon and pepper; cook for 1 minute. Remove from
heat and stir in olive oil. Makes 3½ cups (875 mL).

Fiery Fish Sauce

This sauce can be used for shrimp cocktail; it has been spiced
up from the usual. Serve sauce cold to accompany any cold fish
or brush on top of fillets before baking.

1 cup	ketchup	250 mL
1 tbsp	Worcestershire sauce	15 mL
3 tbsp	freshly grated horseradish (or ⅓ cup/75 mL prepared white horseradish)	50 mL
3 tbsp	lime juice	50 mL
1 tbsp	hot pepper sauce	15 mL
1 tbsp	extra virgin olive oil	15 mL

In 2-cup (500 mL) measure, combine all ingredients. Pour into
glass jar; refrigerate. Makes 1½ cups (375 mL).

New Eggs and Cheese

Skim-Milk Yogurt Cheese

This cheese is very easy to make and can be used in many recipes calling for cream cheese. It can be flavored or spiced, or used plain. The longer the yogurt drains, the thicker it will become, turning into the consistency of cream cheese.

16 oz	skim-milk yogurt	500 g

Place a large basket-type coffee filter into a strainer that can sit in a deep bowl. Pour yogurt into coffee filter; cover strainer with plastic wrap. Refrigerate. Let yogurt drain for 8 to 12 hours. If yogurt is being used for a thick dip, 4 to 8 hours will do. For making cheesecakes or use on bagels, yogurt should drain a minimum of 12 hours.

When the cheese has drained enough, depending on the use, remove it from coffee filter; store in covered container in refrigerator.

Variations:
The following can be added to enhance the taste: honey; sugar substitute; any unsweetened juice concentrate; well-drained unsweetened canned fruit or chopped fresh fruit; any variety of spices or herbs; flavoring extracts; chopped chives or green onions; any chopped dried fruits; raisins and cinnamon. Stir in toasted large-flake oats with fresh, dried or well-drained canned fruit to make a high-energy snack.

NEW EGGS AND CHEESE 73

Cheese and Spinach Spread

This works well for a buffet — great on bagel thins or as a
spread for anything. It can also be a dip for raw vegetables.

1 cup	low-fat (1%) cottage cheese	250 mL
Half	pkg (10 oz/284 g) frozen chopped spinach, thawed and squeezed dry	Half
1 tsp	granulated onion	5 mL
3 tbsp	grated Parmesan cheese	50 mL

In food processor or blender, blend cottage cheese until
smooth. Add spinach; blend until well mixed. Add onion and
Parmesan; mix. The flavor improves if allowed to stand
overnight in refrigerator.

Blue Cheese Spread

The wonderful sharp flavor of blue cheese combines well
with the other ingredients. Only a small amount of cheese is
used, so the fat content is considerably reduced.

8 oz	light cream cheese	250 g
3 tbsp	blue cheese	50 mL
2 to 3 tbsp	dry white wine	25 to 50 mL
1/4 tsp	granulated garlic	1 mL

Using electric beater, blend all ingredients together; adjust
liquid amount to obtain proper consistency for spreading or
dipping. The flavor improves if allowed to stand overnight in
refrigerator.

Macaroni and Cheese

This macaroni and cheese can be a simple side dish, or it can become a whole meal with the addition of fish or meat. A salad or a variety of crisp raw vegetables will go well with this. Older Cheddar cheese gives more flavor, therefore allowing you to use less.

2 cups	uncooked elbow macaroni	500 mL
1 cup	instant skim-milk powder	250 mL
2 cups	water	500 mL
3 tbsp	all-purpose flour	50 mL
¼ cup	water	50 mL
1½ cups	shredded extra-old low-sodium Cheddar	375 mL
1 tsp	dry mustard	5 mL
½ tsp	freshly ground green peppercorns	2 mL
2 tsp	granulated onion	10 mL
3 tbsp	grated Parmesan cheese	50 mL

In pot of boiling water, cook macaroni until al dente (tender but firm); drain. Set aside. In bowl, dissolve skim-milk powder in 2 cups (500 mL) water; pour into 8-cup (2 L) oven-proof casserole.

Dissolve flour in the ¼ cup (50 mL) water; stir into milk. Add Cheddar, dry mustard, peppercorns and onion; blend. Mix in cooked macaroni. Bake, covered, in 350°F (180°C) oven for 30 minutes. Remove from oven and sprinkle with Parmesan. Return to oven; broil, uncovered, until top has browned. Makes 6 to 8 servings.

Variations:
Mix into the cooked macaroni when assembling the casserole: 1 cup (250 mL) leftover chopped meat, chicken, or a can of well-drained, low-sodium, water-packed tuna or salmon.

Basic Omelet

The non-stick pan has gone a long way to make omelets easier for the novice to make, as well as reducing the need for oils and fats. The liquid-egg substitute controversy still rages on. Since this replacement has a high fat content, it is not much better than whole eggs. There are other ways of dealing with reducing the cholesterol found in the yolk of the egg. In larger omelets containing 4 or more eggs, some, in fact most, of the yolks can be left out and all the whites used. This is a handy method for lowering the cholesterol while still enjoying the fresh taste of whole eggs.

For an absolutely plain omelet, the eggs should be beaten with a little water or skim milk, and whipped lightly with a wire whisk just before cooking. A very small amount of vegetable spray is sufficient when using a non-stick pan.

Before the egg is poured into the pan, the surface of the pan should be heated on high. After the egg has been poured into the pan, reduce the heat to medium. As the omelet is setting, loosen the edges with a spatula. When the top is still a bit creamy, slip the spatula under one half and turn it over onto the other half. Continue to cook for 1 minute to set. Serve at once.

Notes:

Use a larger pan to make a thinner omelet, especially when stuffings or fillings are being used.

When making an omelet for 1 serving, 2 eggs are usually used. A large omelet for 3 people can be made with 4 to 5 eggs in a 10- or 12-inch (25 cm or 30 cm) skillet; also include small amounts of cheese, vegetables, meats or fish. To reduce cholesterol when using real eggs, 1 whole egg + 1 egg white + 1 tbsp (15 mL) skim milk can substitute for 2 whole eggs. Very tasty omelets can be made with just egg whites and low-fat cottage cheese, vegetables and spices.

Fillings for Omelets

Fillings can be prepared separately — cooked at the bottom of the pan for those needing more cooking before the egg is poured in, or cooked on top of the omelet for soft or precooked vegetables before folding. Some fillings can be frozen and thawed just before using. Each of the following fillings makes 1 large omelet.

- Cheese Filling: Add ½ tsp (2 mL) onion powder to egg mixture. After egg is poured into pan, sprinkle with 3 to 4 tbsp (50 mL to 60 mL) grated cheese.
- Cheese and Onion Filling: Sauté ½ finely chopped onion before adding eggs. Sprinkle 3 to 4 tbsp (50 mL to 60 mL) grated low-fat cheese on top surface after egg is poured into pan.
- Parmesan and Garlic Filling: Sauté 3 to 4 cloves of garlic finely minced; then pour in egg. Sprinkle 3 to 4 tbsp (50 mL to 60 mL) grated Parmesan cheese over surface.
- Cheese and Mushroom Filling: Sauté 5 sliced mushrooms; pour egg into pan. Sprinkle 3 to 4 tbsp (50 mL to 60 mL) grated low-fat cheese over surface.
- Cheese and Chives Filling: Mix into eggs: ⅓ cup (75 mL) chopped fresh chives or 3 tbsp (50 mL) dried. After egg is poured in pan, sprinkle 3 to 4 tbsp (50 mL to 60 mL) grated low-fat cheese over surface.

Any leftover cooked vegetables, meats and cheeses can easily be used to create a terrific omelet. Macaroni or precooked grains will add interest and texture. Or use leftover cooked or low-sodium canned fish. With any of the cheese combinations above, skim cottage cheese may be substituted.

Any fresh or dried herb may be sprinkled (sparingly) over any omelet before it is folded.

Italian Macaroni Omelet

1 cup	cooked elbow macaroni or other small type	250 mL
3	eggs (or 1 whole egg + 3 whites)	3
2 tbsp	skim milk	25 mL
¼ cup	low-fat (1%) cottage cheese	50 mL
¼ cup	shredded skim-milk mozzarella cheese	50 mL
¼ cup	chopped lean low-sodium ham	50 mL
1 tsp	granulated garlic	5 mL
1 tsp	granulated onion	5 mL
1 tsp	Italian herbs	5 mL
3 tbsp	grated Parmesan cheese	50 mL

In a large bowl, mix together all ingredients except Parmesan cheese. Heat large oven-proof skillet on high with vegetable spray; when hot, pour pasta mixture into pan. Reduce heat to medium; stir mixture so that eggs cook evenly. Cook omelet just until set. Sprinkle Parmesan over surface. Place skillet under hot broiler, about 4 inches (10 cm) away from heat. Broil until top is set and browned. Serve hot or cold. Makes 4 servings.

Baked Italian Omelet

1	small onion, chopped	1
1 tbsp	virgin olive oil	15 mL
¼ lb	mushrooms, sliced	125 g
1	pkg (10 oz/284 g) frozen chopped spinach, thawed and squeezed dry	1
4	eggs (or 1 whole egg + 4 whites)	4
1 tsp	granulated garlic	5 mL
2 tsp	Italian herbs	10 mL
Pinch	white pepper	Pinch
½ cup	low-fat (1%) cottage cheese	125 mL
3 tbsp	grated Parmesan cheese	50 mL

In large oven-proof skillet, brown the onions with olive oil for about 5 minutes. Stir in mushrooms and spinach. Cook for 2 minutes.

In bowl, whisk together eggs, garlic, Italian spices and pepper. Add cottage cheese, mixing well. Pour egg mixture over cooked vegetables in skillet; cook for 5 to 8 minutes, stirring at beginning to make sure eggs cook evenly. When eggs are almost set, sprinkle top of omelet with Parmesan. Place skillet under hot broiler about 4 inches (10 cm) from heat. Broil for 2 to 3 minutes until top is set and cheese is golden brown. Makes 3 to 4 servings.

Tofu and Egg Scramble

This combination is a high-protein treat.

1	cake tofu	1
4	eggs (or 1 whole egg + 4 whites)	4
3 tbsp	skim milk	50 mL
½ tsp	granulated garlic	2 mL
2 tbsp	low-sodium soy sauce	25 mL
1	small onion, chopped	1
3 to 4	mushrooms, sliced	3 to 4

Drain tofu; chop into small chunks. In bowl, beat eggs; add milk, garlic and soy sauce. In large non-stick skillet sprayed with vegetable spray, sauté onion. Add tofu and mushrooms; sauté for 2 minutes. Stir egg mixture; pour into skillet. It takes very little time for eggs to cook; do not overcook. Eggs should be fluffy and wet-looking. Makes 3 to 4 servings.

Blueberry Custard Pancake

This oven-baked pancake is easy and wonderful for a Sunday brunch, or delightful for a light dinner. White rum is used with blueberries in many recipes. Do not substitute, as the rum has a unique effect on the flavor.

1½ cups	fresh or frozen unsweetened blueberries	375 mL
1 tsp	grated lemon rind	5 mL
1 tbsp	white rum	15 mL
4	eggs (or 2 whole eggs + 3 whites)	4
2 cups	skim milk	500 mL
2 tbsp	(heaping) low-fat (1%) yogurt	25 mL
1 tsp	pure vanilla	5 mL
¾ cup	all-purpose flour	175 mL
¼ cup	granulated sugar	50 mL
	Cinnamon	
	Icing sugar	

In bowl, combine blueberries, lemon rind and rum; set aside.

Using wire whisk, beat eggs with ¼ cup (50 mL) of the milk, yogurt, vanilla, flour and granulated sugar. Beat well until frothy. Beat in remaining milk. Spray large oven-proof skillet with vegetable spray; heat on top of stove. Pour batter into hot skillet; sprinkle 1 cup (250 mL) of the blueberries over batter. Place skillet in 450°F (230°C) oven; bake for 20 minutes.

Remove pancake from oven; sprinkle with cinnamon to taste and remaining blueberries. Return pancake to oven; bake for 10 to 15 minutes longer. Sprinkle with icing sugar. Serve hot. Makes 4 to 5 servings.

Variations:
• ½ cup (125 mL) puréed tofu, or 1 cake of well-drained puréed tofu, may be added to the batter to increase the protein.
• Sprinkle 2 tbsp (25 mL) brown sugar over the top of the pancake with the first batch of blueberries.

Baked French Toast

Wonderful, and easy to serve to your family or a large crowd for brunch. Try some of the fruit toppings.

2	eggs (or 1 whole egg + 2 whites)	2
1¼ cups	skim milk	300 mL
1 tsp	pure vanilla	5 mL
1 tbsp	brandy or brandy extract	15 mL
6	thick slices (1 to 1¼ inches/ 2.5 to 3 cm) stale or day-old French bread	6
1 tsp	cinnamon	5 mL
1 tsp	granulated sugar	5 mL
	Icing sugar	

Using wire whisk, beat eggs, milk, vanilla and brandy until well blended and frothy.

Place bread slices into shallow flat pan or dish. Pour over egg mixture; let stand 15 minutes, turning once. The egg mixture should be all absorbed by the bread.

Spray bottom of oven-proof baking pan well with vegetable spray. Place egg-soaked bread into prepared pan. Combine cinnamon and sugar; sprinkle over bread. Bake in 400°F (200°C) oven for 25 minutes or until well browned and puffy. Sprinkle with icing sugar. Makes 6 servings.

Variations:
Serve plain, with maple syrup, low-cal syrup or with your favorite topping (try some of the fruit toppings that follow). For a large group, increase recipe as required and keep French toast in a warm oven until serving time.

Sauces and Other Toppings to Serve with Baked French Toast
• Fresh blueberries or sliced strawberries cooked in a small amount of water or fruit juice; thicken with cornstarch.
• Thin slices of banana.
• 1 cup (250 mL) poached apple slices mixed with 1 tsp (5 mL)

cinnamon, 1 tbsp (15 mL) brandy and 1 tbsp (15 mL) brown sugar.
• Peaches poached with brown sugar and brandy.
• Pears poached in white wine.
• Raspberries, cooked and put through a strainer to remove the seeds; heat, and adjust the sweetness with a small amount of brown sugar.
• Homemade Super Chunky Applesauce (pg. 215) served warm.

The Great Pancake

This is a great basic pancake; the batter can also be used for waffles if you have a waffle iron. Since I developed this recipe many years ago, we no longer go out in search of the Great Pancake. This is it.

2 cups	all-purpose flour	500 mL
1 tbsp	baking powder	15 mL
1 tbsp	granulated sugar	15 mL
½ cup	low-fat yogurt	125 mL
1 tsp	baking soda	5 mL
1½ cups	(approx) skim milk	375 mL
1	egg, beaten (or 2 egg whites)	1
1 tbsp	canola oil	15 mL

In large plastic pitcher, mix flour, baking powder and sugar. In 1-cup (250 mL) measure, combine yogurt with soda; let it foam.

In large measuring cup, mix milk, egg and oil until blended.

Add wet ingredients to dry ingredients in pitcher. Using long-handled wooden spoon, mix until blended. Batter should be thick and lumpy. As batter sits, it will get a bit thicker and can be thinned slightly with skim milk. The batter should be the consistency of very thick cream.

Heat large skillet or griddle. Coat with vegetable spray to restrict calories; or small amounts (1 tbsp/15 mL as needed) of canola oil may be used. For each pancake, pour about ¼ cup to 1/3 cup (50 mL to 75 mL) batter into skillet. When many bubbles appear on surface of pancake, turn pancake. Makes 8 to 10 pancakes.

Notes:
• Never flip a pancake more than once or it will become tough.
• This recipe can be doubled for larger groups. Leftover batter can be kept in the refrigerator for several days or frozen. Freeze leftover pancakes with waxed paper between each, in a plastic bag. Heat in a toaster oven for a fast breakfast.

Variations:
Any of the following may be added to the basic pancake batter:
• ½ cup (125 mL) tiny chocolate chips.
• 1 cup (250 mL) fresh or frozen unsweetened blueberries.
• 1 cup (250 mL) chopped fresh peaches, strawberries, bananas, kiwi.
• 1 large unpeeled apple, grated, and 1 tsp (5 mL) cinnamon.
• 1 cup (250 mL) cranberries, chopped.
• ½ cup (125 mL) peanut butter chips.
Replace ½ cup (125 mL) of the all-purpose flour with an equal amount of one of the following: oat bran, quick-cooking rolled oats, rice flour, whole-wheat flour, rye flour, corn flour, all-bran cereal (soaked in some of the milk to soften), buckwheat flour.

Flavoring variations:
Reduce the skim milk by ½ cup (125 mL) and add ½ cup (125 mL) unsweetened orange juice. Add grated peel from 1 orange. Omit granulated sugar.

Sourdough Pancakes

Try these pancakes for a new taste. All the variations that appear after The Great Pancake (pg. 81) may be used here.

2 cups	all-purpose flour	500 mL
1 tsp	baking powder	5 mL
1 tbsp	granulated sugar	15 mL
1	egg, beaten (or 2 egg whites)	1
1 tbsp	canola oil	15 mL
1 cup	sourdough starter (see pp. 184-186)	250 mL
½ cup	low-fat (1%) yogurt	125 mL
½ tsp	baking soda	2 mL

In large plastic pitcher, mix flour, baking powder, sugar, egg, oil and sourdough starter. In separate bowl, blend yogurt with baking soda; when it foams add to the batter. Using long-handled wooden or plastic (not metal) spoon, mix batter until thick and lumpy. Let stand for 10 minutes. Check consistency before using, adding skim milk if it is very thick.

Heat skillet or griddle. Coat with vegetable spray. For each pancake, pour ¼ cup to ⅓ cup (50 mL to 75 mL) of batter into skillet. Flip pancake when many bubbles appear and break the surface. Makes 8 to 10 pancakes.

Baked Apple Custard Pancake

This baked pancake is similar to the Blueberry Custard Pancake; however, the method is not quite the same. Great for brunch or a light meal.

1 tbsp	margarine	15 mL
2	large apples, peeled, cored and thinly sliced	2
3 tbsp	lemon juice	50 mL
½ tsp	(approx) cinnamon	2 mL
1½ tsp	brandy	7 mL
1½ tsp	brown sugar	7 mL
4	eggs, well beaten (or 1 whole egg + 4 whites)	4
2 cups	skim milk	500 mL
2 tbsp	(heaping) low-fat (1%) yogurt	25 mL
1 tsp	pure vanilla	5 mL
¼ cup	granulated sugar	50 mL
¾ cup	all-purpose flour Icing sugar (optional)	175 mL

In 10-cup (2.5 L) oven-proof skillet, combine margarine, apples, lemon juice, cinnamon, brandy and brown sugar; mix well to coat apples. Cook over medium heat for 3 to 4 minutes. Apples should be soft but not mushy. Remove from heat; set aside.

In bowl, combine eggs, ¼ cup (50 mL) of the milk, yogurt, vanilla, granulated sugar and flour. Beat well with wire whisk until frothy. Add remaining milk; beat again. Pour batter over prepared apples in skillet; bake in 425°F (220°C) oven for 30 to 35 minutes until pancake is golden and puffy.

Remove from oven; invert pancake over platter. Sprinkle with extra cinnamon. A sprinkle of icing sugar is decorative, but optional. Serve hot. Makes 4 to 5 servings.

Simply Delicious Fish

How to Determine Cooking Time for Fish

The best and most reliable timing method for fish is the one developed by the Canadian Department of Fisheries for baking, broiling, poaching, sautéing, steaming, even frying. Lay the fish on a flat surface; measure its thickest point. For each inch (2.5 cm) of thickness, allow 10 minutes of cooking time. (This does not apply to fish to be cooked in soups and stews.) Measure the thickness of rolled fillets *after* you have rolled them. All cooking should be done as quickly as possible over high heat to preserve the full flavor and texture of the fish.

Although this method is a trusty guide, always check the fish to be sure it is done and to prevent overcooking. Stick a skewer into the thick flesh behind the gills of a whole fish; the skewer should slide in easily. Prick the flesh of fillets or steaks with a fork; the flesh should barely flake.

When cooking still-frozen fish, double the cooking time indicated by the thickness of the fish.

When freezing fresh fish, dip the rinsed fish in lightly salted water; wrap and seal. Freeze lean fish for up to 6 months, fat fish for 3 months. Thaw fish only when you will be using it.

Baked Fish

If a sauce is being used on the fish while it is being baked, add 5 minutes to the cooking time. Saucing may also be done after the fish has cooked. Before baking stuffed fillets or steaks, spread the stuffing over the fish and measure the total thickness (fish plus stuffing) to determine the cooking time.

When baking fresh fish in foil, allow an extra 5 minutes of cooking time per inch (2.5 cm) of thickness, and an extra 10 minutes of cooking time for frozen fish baked in foil.

Basic Fish Baked in a Covered Dish

1½ lb	fish (any type fillet or steak)	750 g
1½ tsp	extra virgin olive oil	7 mL
3 tbsp	dry white wine	50 mL
	Sprinkling of freshly ground green peppercorns	
	Lemon slices	
	Finely chopped parsley	
2	large carrots, peeled and sliced into rounds	2

Arrange fish in baking dish; brush fish with olive oil. Add wine. Sprinkle fish with ground peppercorns. Lay lemon slices over fish. Sprinkle with parsley. Place carrots over and beside fish. Bake in 350°F (180°C) oven for length of time according to thickness of fish. Makes 4 servings.

Basic Fish Baked in Foil

1½ lb	thick-cut fish (any type)	750 g
2	green onions or dillweed, finely chopped	2
8	cloves garlic, peeled	8
	Sprinkling of freshly ground pepper	
	Sprinkling of celery seed	
	Thinly sliced lemon	

Cut a sheet of heavy-duty aluminum foil large enough to fold over fish and crimp together. Spray dull side of foil with vegetable spray. Place fish on foil; cover with green onions, garlic, pepper, celery seed and lemon. Bring sides of foil together, folding to seal; crimp ends closed. Bake in 350°F (180°C) oven for length of time according to thickness of fish. Makes 4 servings.

Baked Fish Italian Style

1½ lb	fish fillets or steaks	750 g
1½ tsp	extra virgin olive oil	7 mL
3 tbsp	dry white wine	50 mL
2	small or 1 large tomato, thinly sliced	2
3	large cloves garlic, sliced	3
1 tsp	granulated onion	5 mL
1 tbsp	Italian herbs	15 mL
3 tbsp	grated Parmesan cheese	50 mL

Arrange fish in baking dish. Brush fish with olive oil.
Sprinkle wine over fish. Arrange tomato slices over fish; add
garlic. Sprinkle fish with onion, Italian herbs and cheese.
Bake, covered, in 450°F (230°C) oven for length of time
according to thickness of fish. Makes 4 servings.

Chinese Baked Fish

1½ lb	fish fillets or steaks	750 g
1 tbsp	cornstarch	15 mL
3 tbsp	water	50 mL
1½ tsp	sesame seed oil	7 mL
2	green onions, chopped	2
3 tbsp	low-sodium soy sauce	50 mL
2 tbsp	dry white wine	25 mL
2 tbsp	lemon juice	25 mL
½ tsp	granulated garlic	2 mL
½ tsp	ground ginger	2 mL
	Thin lemon slices	

Arrange fish in baking dish. In bowl, mix cornstarch with
water. Add sesame oil, green onions, soy sauce, wine, lemon
juice, garlic and ginger; blend well. Pour sauce over fish.
Arrange lemon slices on top of fish. Bake, covered, in 450°F
(230°C) oven for length of time according to thickness of fish.
Makes 4 servings.

Fish Baked in Beer

4	green onions, finely chopped	4
1½ lb	fish fillets or steaks	750 g
½ cup	light beer	250 mL
¼ cup	finely chopped fresh parsley	50 mL
	White pepper	
	Onion powder	
	Garlic powder	
	Crushed tarragon	

Place green onions in baking dish. Arrange fish on top; pour in beer. Sprinkle with parsley and seasonings to taste.

Bake, covered, in 350°F (180°C) oven for length of time according to thickness of fish. Makes 4 servings.

Fish Baked in Tomato Basil with Cognac

1½ lb	fish fillets or steaks	750 g
2 tbsp	cognac	25 mL
2	tomatoes, thinly sliced	2
1 tsp	granulated garlic	5 mL
1½ tsp	dried basil	7 mL
Pinch	freshly ground pepper	Pinch
2 tbsp	grated Parmesan cheese	25 mL

Arrange fish in baking dish; sprinkle with cognac. Cover with tomato slices. Sprinkle with remaining ingredients. Bake, covered, in 450°F (230°C) oven for length of time according to thickness of fish. Makes 4 servings.

Barbecued Fish

Fat-fleshed fish are the best for the barbecue. Lean-fleshed fish are less successful unless they are carefully wrapped in foil to prevent the fish from drying out. Very delicate-fleshed fish should not be barbecued.

Barbecue large whole fish in a greased wire cage. Small mesh-type cooking surfaces are made for holding fish on the barbecue; they also work well for anything small that might fall through the grill. Fillets and steaks should be cut thick, at least 1/2 inch (1 cm); turn them only once.

Barbecue for length of time according to thickness of fish.

Grilling Fish in Foil

1½ lb	lean fish fillets or steaks (or 1 to 3 lb/500 g to 1.5 kg whole fish, cleaned, dried and dressed)	750 g
1 tbsp	extra virgin olive oil	15 mL
⅓ cup	dry white wine	75 mL
2	large cloves garlic, chopped (or 2 tsp/10 mL granulated garlic)	2
2	green onions, finely chopped	2
2 tsp	dried tarragon	10 mL
1 tsp	thyme	5 mL

Arrange fish on double thickness of heavy-duty foil, allowing enough extra foil to fold over and seal. (NOTE: a foil baking pan may be used instead, with a cover of foil.)

In bowl, blend together well remaining ingredients; pour sauce over fish. Bring edges of foil together, sealing tightly. Grill fish about 4 inches (10 cm) from coals, for length of time according to thickness of fish. Makes 4 servings.

Barbecued Fish Steaks

4	fish steaks, 3/4-inch to 1-inch (2 cm to 2.5 cm) thick	4
1 tbsp	extra virgin olive oil	15 mL
1/2 cup	dry white wine	125 mL
1/4 cup	lemon juice	50 mL
3 tbsp	finely chopped fresh parsley	50 mL
Pinch	white pepper	Pinch
1 tsp	dried thyme	5 mL
	Lemon wedges	

Wash steaks, dry with paper towel and arrange in one layer in shallow dish. In large measuring cup, blend well oil, wine, lemon juice, parsley, pepper and thyme; pour marinade over fish. Refrigerate for 4 hours, turning occasionally. Remove fish; place it on greased rack about 4 inches (10 cm) above coals. Barbecue, turning the fish once, for length of time according to thickness of fish. (Baste with marinade during cooking.) Serve with lemon wedges.

Note:
The fish can be marinated the night before and kept refrigerated until ready to grill the next day.

Broiled Fish
All types of fish can be broiled. Lean-fleshed fish will need to be gently brushed with a very small amount of oil or a basting sauce before broiling. Fat-fleshed fish will not require any extra attention. Broiled fish is best seasoned after it is cooked.

When broiling fish, preheat the broiler for 10 minutes and time the cooking according to the thickness of the fish. Use a rack sprayed with vegetable spray, and place the fish 2 to 4 inches (5 cm to 10 cm) away from the broiler. If the fish is frozen, place it about 6 inches (15 cm) away to prevent overcooking the surface before the inside is done. Only thick fish cuts need to be turned; thin ones may be broiled without turning.

Sauces for Basting Broiled Fish

1. Mix together: 1 tbsp (15 mL) walnut oil, 2 tbsp (25 mL) lemon juice, pinch of white pepper. Baste fish. Baste again halfway through broiling.

2. Mix together: 1 tbsp (15 mL) extra virgin olive oil, 2 tbsp (25 mL) lemon juice, 1 tbsp (15 mL) Dijon mustard, pinch of white pepper, pinch of garlic powder. Baste fish. Baste again halfway through broiling.

3. Mix together: 1 tbsp (15 mL) sesame seed oil, 2 tbsp (25 mL) low-sodium soy sauce, 1 tbsp (15 mL) dry white wine, 1 tsp (5 mL) cornstarch mixed with 2 tsp (10 mL) lemon juice, ½ tsp (2 mL) garlic powder, 2 tbsp (25 mL) chopped green onions. Baste fish. Baste again halfway through broiling.

4. Mix together: 2 tbsp (25 mL) Dijon mustard, 1 tbsp (15 mL) light mayonnaise, 1 tbsp (15 mL) dry white wine, pinch of white pepper, pinch of ground celery seed. Baste fish. Baste again halfway through broiling.

Poaching Fish

Poaching is an ideal method for cooking lean fish. Whole fish are generally poached with the head and tail on, but dressed and scaled. A wrapping of cheesecloth will make lifting the fish in and out of the poaching liquid easier. Smaller fillets or steaks may be lifted out with a broad turner or spatula.

Fish may be poached in water, milk or a court bouillon. Strain and reserve the liquid to make sauces or soups.

When poaching, bring the liquid to a boil, and place the fish in it. The liquid should barely cover the fish. When the liquid returns nearly to the boil, begin to time the cooking according to the thickness of the fish.

Poached Fish in Vegetable Broth

1½ lb	fish fillets, cut in serving pieces or steaks	750 g
2 to 3	carrots, peeled and cut into 2-inch (5 cm) pieces	2 to 3
2	large stalks celery, cut into 3-inch (8 cm) pieces	2
1	onion, thickly sliced	1
2	cloves garlic, chopped	2
1 tbsp	lemon juice	15 mL
2 cups	water	500 mL
¼ cup	dry white wine	50 mL
1 tsp	whole peppercorns	5 mL
1 tbsp	dried tarragon	15 mL

In a poacher or other container large enough to hold fish in a single layer, place all ingredients except fish; bring mixture to a boil. Cook over medium heat until vegetables are softened but still crisp, about 10 minutes.

Add fish to cooking liquid. When liquid returns nearly to a boil, start timing cooking according to thickness of fish.

Remove fish to serving platter. The vegetables may be served with the fish. The cooking liquid may be thickened and used for a sauce on the fish. Makes 4 servings.

Sautéed Fish

All types of fish may be sautéed, but it is best to use fillets, steaks or small whole fish that are dressed. Large pieces of fish are difficult to remove from the pan without breaking.

Fish can be sautéed using several methods. Basically, the fish is dipped into a liquid — whole egg, egg white, milk or wine — then rolled lightly in seasoned flour, cornmeal, crushed cornflakes, toasted oats or breadcrumbs.

The skillet should be well heated before any fish is added. I recommend using a very minimal amount of oil, for the flavor and to maintain the moistness of lean fish. A non-stick skillet does a wonderful job; oil can be totally eliminated and the fish dry-fried. (Oil can also be eliminated when a fat-fleshed fish is used.) A light coat of olive oil spray adds flavor and is sparing on calories.

The cooking time is calculated by the thickness of the fish. When sautéing, divide the time in half for each side, and flip the fish only once to avoid damaging it.

Lemon and parsley are nice over sautéed fish. Almost any sauce can be served on or with this fish.

Basic Sautéed Fish with Crunchy Coatings

This has always been my children's favorite way of eating fish, and for many years when they were young, the only way. Vary the coatings to change the taste. Any fish can be used — children tend to like sole (lack of bones) or any similar fish the best. Make a large quantity; the kids seem to really like this one. Leftovers can be wrapped and frozen, or eaten cold the next day. I recommend Fiery Fish Sauce (pg. 71), though my children prefer Barbecue Sauce (pg. 64).

2 lb	fish fillets or steaks, cut into 8 serving pieces	1 kg
1	egg beaten with 2 tbsp (25 mL) water (or 2 egg whites beaten with 2 tbsp/25 mL water)	1
1 to 2 tbsp	canola oil or olive oil pan spray	15 to 25 mL
	Bread crumb Coating (pg. 94), Ground Toasted Oat Coating (pg. 94), Flour Coating (pg. 95) or Cornflake Coating (pg. 95)	

Wash fish and dry well. Dip fish on both sides in egg mixture. Place fish into coating mixture, pressing fish gently into mixture to coat both sides well.

In skillet, heat 1 tbsp (15 mL) of the oil. Sauté the fish on one side for half the cooking time required according to thickness of fish. Turn fish; sauté for remaining time. Add remaining oil as needed. Undercook fish slightly if it will be heated before serving. Transfer fish to serving platter.

Note:
This fish heats well in the microwave oven, allowing it to be cooked long before serving. If reheating is done in a regular oven, be sure to cover the container to prevent the fish from drying out.

Bread Crumb Coating

1 cup	dry bread crumbs	250 mL
¼ cup	grated Parmesan cheese	50 mL
2 tsp	Season All	10 mL
2 tsp	granulated onion	10 mL
2 tsp	granulated garlic	10 mL
½ tsp	white pepper	2 mL

Mix all ingredients together; pour on flat dish or waxed paper, ready for coating fish. Makes enough to coat 8 medium fish pieces.

Ground Toasted Oat Coating

1 cup	ground toasted oats	250 mL
1½ tsp	garlic powder	7 mL
1½ tsp	onion powder	7 mL
1½ tsp	crumbled dried parsley	7 mL

Mix all ingredients together; pour on flat dish or waxed
paper, ready for coating fish. Makes enough to coat 8 medium
fish pieces.

Flour Coating

½ cup	all-purpose flour	125 mL
1 tsp	granulated garlic	5 mL
1 tsp	granulated onion	5 mL
1 tsp	white pepper	5 mL
½ tsp	Season All	2 mL

Mix all ingredients together; pour on flat dish or waxed
paper, ready for coating fish. Makes enough to coat 8 medium
fish pieces.

Cornflake Coating

1 cup	crushed cornflakes	250 mL
2 tsp	granulated onion	10 mL
2 tsp	granulated garlic	10 mL
½ tsp	white pepper	2 mL
2 tsp	Season All	10 mL
¼ cup	grated Parmesan cheese	50 mL

Mix all ingredients together; pour on flat dish or waxed
paper, ready for coating fish. Makes enough to coat 8 medium
fish pieces.

Canned Fish

Availability of canned tuna and salmon makes these dishes
easy and economical. I recommend using water-packed low-
sodium fish. Check the recipe first before discarding the

water from the can. In the event that water-packed is not available, drain the liquid from the fish, rinse the fish in cold water and drain on absorbent paper. Removing skin and bones from the salmon is optional.

Canned fish adapts well to any use with pasta for a quick and nutritious meal. Tuna or salmon may be substituted for meat or chicken in many of the pasta recipes in this book.

Do not limit yourself to tuna and salmon; a can of shrimp, for example, will make a great dinner salad with one of the dressings in the salad section.

Salmon or Tuna Patties

These patties make a terrific dinner with macaroni and cheese and a green vegetable. Try Fiery Fish Sauce (pg. 71) or Barbecue Sauce (pg. 64).

2	cans (each 7½ oz/213 mL) water-packed, low-sodium salmon or tuna	2
½ cup	bread crumbs	125 mL
¼ cup	instant skim-milk powder	50 mL
¼ cup	water	50 mL
1	egg (or 2 egg whites)	1
2 tsp	Dijon mustard	10 mL
2 tsp	granulated onion	10 mL
¼ tsp	white pepper	1 mL
2 tbsp	prepared white horseradish	25 mL

Drain salmon or tuna. In bowl, mash fish. Add remaining ingredients, mixing well after each addition. Make patties.

In non-stick skillet sprayed with olive oil spray, sauté patties on each side to brown. Remove to serving platter. They may be frozen when cool, or refrigerated and reheated in microwave oven or toaster oven.

Variation:
Substitute for the bread crumbs: ½ cup to ¾ cup (125 mL to 175 mL) cooked leftover mashed potato or the same quantity of instant mashed potato flakes.

Salmon and Broccoli Bake

1	bunch broccoli, coarsely chopped	1
2 tbsp	canola oil	25 mL
2 tbsp	all-purpose flour	25 mL
2 cups	skim milk	500 mL
¼ cup	grated Parmesan cheese	50 mL
3 tbsp	shredded extra-old low-fat Cheddar cheese	50 mL
½ tsp	dry mustard	2 mL
1 tsp	granulated onion	5 mL
Pinch	white pepper	Pinch
1 tbsp	lemon juice	15 mL
2	cans (each 7½ oz/213 mL) salmon, skin and bones removed (liquid reserved)	2
6 tbsp	toasted rolled oats	90 mL

Place broccoli in shallow casserole.

In saucepan over medium heat, pour in oil; add flour, blending well. Add milk slowly, stirring constantly until thickened and bubbling.

Stir in Parmesan, Cheddar, mustard, onion, pepper, lemon juice and reserved juice from salmon. Cook for 1 minute. Stir in salmon. Pour mixture over broccoli. Sprinkle with oats. Bake in 400°F (200°C) oven for 15 to 20 minutes. Makes 4 to 5 servings.

Center Stage for the New Ground Meats

Ground Meats

Ground meat has come a long way since the days of the greasy hamburger. Consumer demand has improved the availability of lean and extra-lean ground meats. Ask at the store where you purchase ground meats for the percentage of fat in the various types. Ten percent or less fat is considered extra-lean; 10 to 15% is lean. Stay with the lowest fat content possible. For those people who want or require ground meat without any fat, the only way is to grind the meat at home. Some butchers and supermarkets will custom-grind any cut of meat for you, and it can be done with little or no fat.

Ground meat without fat can be very dry and have little taste. Since the fat that gives ground meat its flavor and moisture is missing, other ingredients must be added.

Ground meat has traditionally been beef, but a variety of ground meats are gaining popularity. Veal, chicken and turkey will add new flavor and dimension to a meal. (Pork is not included here, as it is high in fat and calories.)

Ground meats also lend themselves well to pre-prepared meals for active life-styles, and for meals to serve one or two. Fresh ground meat of any variety can be prepared and made into individual patties. Wrap each separately in a piece of waxed paper. Stack them up, place in a plastic freezer bag, seal and freeze. Remove one or more anytime for a quick and easy meal. Meatballs can also be prepared in quantity before use; however, they are easier to store when cooked, cooled, then bagged in freezer bags and sealed tightly.

Ground meats can become many other creative shapes and part of other combinations — as a loaf, with a stuffing, or as a stuffing for something else. In the recipes that follow, I provide numerous ways to improve the taste, texture and moisture content of ground meats. All the meats used here are extra-lean, or ground without fat.

Better-than-Ever Hamburger

Since the quantity of meat that is used will vary from time to time, the amount of flavorings and other additions is approximate, based on 1 lb (500 g) of meat. The ground meat used can be a combination of two or more types, or just one.

1 lb	extra-lean ground meat	500 g
1	egg (or 2 egg whites) (Note: to a maximum of 3 eggs or 5 whites for up to 5 lb/2.2 kg of meat)	1
½ cup	unsweetened applesauce	125 mL
2 tbsp	Worcestershire sauce	25 mL
3 tbsp	prepared mustard	50 mL
3 tbsp	ketchup	50 mL
½ cup	bread crumbs	125 mL
¼ cup	(approx) water (adjust for meat to hold together and handle easily)	50 mL
2 tsp	granulated onion	10 mL
2 tsp	granulated garlic	10 mL
2 tsp	Season All	10 mL
1 tsp	freshly ground black pepper	5 mL

In large bowl, mix all ingredients well. Form meat into patties. Burgers can be: cooked in non-stick skillet with no added fats broiled in oven; or barbecued on grill.

Variations:
A great method to stretch minced meats and keep a high protein level without adding cholesterol is to mix tofu into the meat. For every 1 lb (500 g) meat, add ½ cup to ¾ cup (125 mL to 175 mL) drained and mashed tofu. The tofu can also be puréed first, then blended in with meat. The egg may be omitted when using tofu.

The applesauce may be omitted, and water or other liquid such as broth, sauce or wine may be used to increase the moisture level (the amount may vary). However, the applesauce does add fiber to your diet.

Italian Burgers

1 lb	extra-lean ground meat	500 g
1	egg (or 2 egg whites)	1
¼ cup	thawed frozen chopped spinach (with liquid)	50 mL
¼ cup	bread crumbs	50 mL
1 tbsp	Worcestershire sauce	15 mL
3 tbsp	ketchup	50 mL
3 to 4 tbsp	water or dry red or white wine	50 mL
2 tsp	granulated garlic	10 mL
2 tsp	granulated onion	10 mL
1 to 2 tbsp	chili powder	15 to 25 mL
1 tbsp	Italian herbs	15 mL

In large bowl, mix all ingredients well. Form meat into patties. Burgers can be: cooked in non-stick skillet with no added fats; broiled in oven; or barbecued on grill.

Variation:
Before cooking these burgers, sprinkle with a small amount of grated Parmesan cheese.

Chinese Burgers

1 lb	extra-lean ground meat	500 g
1	egg (or 2 egg whites)	1
¼ cup	bread crumbs	50 mL
2 tbsp	(approx) water or dry white wine	25 mL
2 tbsp	low-sodium soy sauce	25 mL
2 tbsp	prepared mustard	25 mL
1 to 2 tbsp	chopped green onions	15 to 25 mL
½ tsp	ground ginger	2 mL
2 tsp	granulated onion	10 mL
2 tsp	granulated garlic	10 mL

In large bowl, mix all ingredients well. Form meat into patties. Burgers can be cooked in non-stick skillet with no added fats broiled in oven; or barbecued on grill.

Spicy Chili Burgers

Spices can be adjusted on this one if people like it hotter. If only one or two people like it hot, use the spice amounts given here and add extra spice to their burgers while they cook.

1 lb	ground meat	500 g
1	egg (or 2 egg whites)	1
¼ cup	bread crumbs	50 mL
2 tbsp	Worcestershire sauce	25 mL
1 tbsp	Dijon mustard	15 mL
3 tbsp	ketchup	50 mL
1 to 3 tsp	hot pepper sauce	5 to 15 mL
1 to 2 tbsp	chili powder	15 to 25 mL
2 tsp	granulated garlic	10 mL
2 tsp	granulated onion	10 mL
½ tsp	freshly ground pepper	2 mL
2 to 3 tbsp	water or dry white wine	25 to 50 mL

In large bowl, mix all ingredients well. Form meat into patties. Burgers can be: cooked in non-stick skillet with no added fats; broiled in oven; or barbecued on grill.

Teriyaki Turkey Burgers

1 lb	extra-lean ground turkey	500 g
1	egg (or 2 egg whites)	1
¼ cup	dry bread crumbs	50 mL
3 tbsp	finely chopped green onions	50 mL
½ tsp	ground ginger	2 mL
3 tbsp	low-sodium soy sauce	50 mL
2 to 3 tbsp	dry white wine	25 to 50 mL

In large bowl, mix all ingredients well. Form meat into patties. Burgers can be: cooked in non-stick skillet with no added fats; broiled in oven; or barbecued on grill.

Making Pita Burgers

Whatever meat mixture is used, spices and meat combinations can be varied. Before making a regular burger, consider the benefits and possibilities of a pita burger.

Pita has become very popular. It is not hard to see why: pita comes in regular as well as whole-wheat, oat bran and high-fiber. Many grocery stores and delis now carry it. A pita burger is a half-moon-shaped burger tucked into a pita pocket with shredded lettuce, tomatoes, onions, mushrooms, grated cheese, shredded carrots, mustard, peppers, relishes and anything else you want. Try a pita burger — the only thing missing is a large and heavy burger bun. In some areas, a new shape of pita has been showing up, made especially for the round burger. If these are not available, the burger can be made to fit the half-moon shape.

Shape about ¼ lb (125 g) or less of the prepared burger meat into a half circle; place on waxed paper; wrap. Place wrapped burgers into a plastic freezer bag and seal for later use. Or prepare and cook burgers on a dry pan or barbecue grill.

Stuffed Pita Burgers

The half-circle shape of the pita burger means it fits perfectly into a half slice of pita bread.

¼ lb	(or less) burger meat	125 g
2 tbsp	shredded low-fat Cheddar cheese or skim-milk mozzarella	25 g
1	pita pocket	1

Press burger meat into thin circle. On half, place Cheddar cheese; fold other half over cheese. Press and seal edges. (If desired, wrap and freeze.) Burger can be: cooked in non-stick skillet with no added fats; broiled in oven; or barbecued on grill. Place cooked meat in pita pocket. Makes 1 pita burger.

Other Stuffings
• 2 tbsp (25 mL) chopped frozen spinach (thawed, with water squeezed out). Place spinach on half of the thin circle of meat, sprinkle with 1 tsp (5 mL) grated Parmesan cheese, fold over and seal edges.
• 2 tbsp (25 mL) leftover mashed potato, rice, kasha or other cooked grain.
• Sautéed onions or mushrooms, or a combination of both.

Regular Meat Loaf

Using any of the burger mixtures in this chapter, form the meat into a loaf shape. Place in a covered loaf pan. Pour into pan ½ cup (125 mL) water, or wine, or sauce. (See sauces pp. 64-71.) Bake at 350°F (180°C) oven until loaf feels firm on inside. (Test for doneness with a fork inserted into the middle.) Let the loaf stand for 10 minutes before slicing.

Rolled Stuffed Meat Loaf

Stuffing can be made from vegetables or bread. The stuffing can also be another type of ground meat. Leftover mashed potatoes can be used the same way.

A minimum of 2 lb (1 kg) meat should be used. Leftovers can be frozen and used another time. When this loaf is refrigerated, slice it thin and serve cold with a salad or on an open-faced sandwich.

2 lb	burger mixture (see recipes from this chapter)	1 kg
4	slices fresh or day-old bread (rye, oat bran, whole-wheat, pumpernickel or combination)	4
1	onion, finely chopped	1
1	large stalk celery, finely chopped	1
¼ lb	mushrooms, finely chopped	125 g
2 tsp	granulated onion	10 mL
2 tsp	granulated garlic	10 mL
2 tsp	Season All	10 mL
1 tsp	freshly ground pickling spice	5 mL
½ cup	water or dry wine	125 mL

Place prepared burger mixture on large piece of waxed paper; flatten the meat with your hand. Place another piece of waxed paper on top of meat. Gently roll meat flat, using rolling pin, into rectangle, about ½ inch (1 cm) thick. Set aside.

Chop by hand or use food processor to finely process bread.

In pan sprayed with vegetable spray, sauté onion and celery until onion begins to brown. Add onion and celery to bowl containing processed bread.

Sauté mushrooms in pan for only a few moments; do not overcook. Add mushrooms to bread. Blend in onion, garlic, Season All and pickling spice.

Evenly spread bread stuffing over surface of rolled-out meat. Using waxed paper on bottom, start at the long side and roll loaf, pressing the meat tightly as you roll. Smooth ends so stuffing is encased with the outer cover of meat and will not leak out. Place in roasting pan, seam side down. Add water to pan. Bake, covered, in 350°F (180°C) oven for about 15 minutes per pound (500 g) of meat. Halfway through baking, uncover roll. Makes 1 loaf.

Cold Pepper Veal Loaf

This can be served hot as a veal meat loaf, cut in thick pieces. It is fantastic served cold and sliced thin. Use it cold with salads or as cold cuts.

2 to 2½ lb	extra-lean ground veal	1 to 1.25 kg
2	eggs (or 3 egg whites)	2
1 tbsp	granulated onion	15 mL
1 tbsp	granulated garlic	15 mL
1 tbsp	green peppercorns, crushed	15 mL
3 tbsp	Worcestershire sauce	50 mL
⅓ cup	bread crumbs	75 mL
¼ cup	dry white wine	50 mL

In large bowl, mix all ingredients together. Adjust liquid if more is needed to hold meat together well. Shape into 1 large or 2 small loaves; place in baking pan. Bake, uncovered, in 350°F (180°C) oven until loaf is well browned, 40 to 55 minutes. To serve cold, remove from baking pan, wrap, and refrigerate until cold. To serve hot, remove to serving dish, let stand 5 minutes before slicing. Makes 1 large loaf or 2 small loaves.

Turkey Logs

You can adjust the spices to your own tastes.

1 lb	extra-lean ground turkey	500 g
1	egg (or 2 egg whites)	1
2 tbsp	Worcestershire sauce	25 mL
2 tbsp	prepared mustard	25 mL
2 tbsp	ketchup	25 mL
½ cup	bread crumbs	125 mL
¼ cup	light beer or dry white wine or water	50 mL
2 tsp	granulated garlic	10 mL
2 tsp	granulated onion	10 mL
2 tsp	Season All	10 mL
1 tsp	chili powder	5 mL
½ tsp	freshly ground pepper	2 mL

In large bowl, mix all ingredients until well blended. Small amounts of water may be added so meat holds together well. Take about 2 to 3 heaping tablespoons (25 mL to 50 mL) of mixture; roll it in your hands (moistened with water) to form log shape about 2½ inches (6 cm) long. Prepare non-stick skillet with vegetable spray; cook logs over medium heat. (When cooled, logs can be frozen for later use.) Serve with Barbecue Sauce (pg. 64) or make a gravy from fat-skimmed pan drippings. Serves 3 to 4.

Spinach Meatballs with Tomato Sauce

1½ lb	extra-lean ground beef	750 g
1	pkg (10 oz/284 g) frozen chopped spinach, thawed and drained	1
1	onion, finely chopped	1
½ tbsp	granulated garlic	7 mL
3 tbsp	grated Parmesan cheese	50 mL
⅓ cup	dry bread crumbs	75 mL
1	egg (or 2 egg whites)	1
½ tsp	freshly ground pepper	2 mL

1 cup	water	250 mL
2 tbsp	all-purpose flour	25 mL
1	can (28 oz/796 mL) plain (no salt) tomato sauce	1
1 tsp	Worcestershire sauce	15 mL
1 tbsp	dried basil	15 mL
1 tbsp	dried tarragon	15 mL
1 tbsp	granulated garlic	15 mL
1 tbsp	granulated onion	15 mL
¼ cup	dry red or white wine or low-sodium beef broth or water	50 mL
1 tbsp	extra virgin olive oil (optional)	15 mL
	Grated Parmesan cheese (optional)	

In large bowl, mix together beef, spinach, onion, ½ tbsp (7 mL) garlic, 3 tbsp (50 mL) Parmesan, bread crumbs, egg and pepper; shape into meatballs the size of golf balls.

In non-stick skillet, dry-fry (or a light spray of olive oil spray may be used) meatballs until browned but not fully cooked.

Meanwhile, in small bowl, whisk together water and flour. In another bowl, mix tomato sauce, Worcestershire sauce, basil, tarragon, 1 tbsp (15 mL) garlic, onion powder and wine. Blend in flour mixture.

Stir tomato mixture into meatballs in pan. Cook over low heat, stirring until thickened and meatballs have finished cooking, 8 to 10 minutes. At end of cooking, add olive oil, if using, for flavor. Serve with additional Parmesan cheese at the table, if desired. Makes 4 to 5 servings.

Chili

Great chili exists everywhere. Everyone has a favorite recipe. The variations are numerous, and depending on the area in which the chili is made, tastes will vary greatly.

There are, however, a few tried and tested methods of making chili, no matter what combination of ingredients is used.

1. Choose a large pot with a flat bottom. It is best to make chili in a larger quantity than is needed because it improves with age and freezes well.

2. Simmering is a vital part of making chili. Chili should be simmered uncovered to allow the juices to cook down and develop with the spices.

3. In many chili recipes, the fat is considered part of the overall taste, but in my recipes all animal fat will be removed. However, for those who really want some great flavor without the saturated fat, here's a tip: After the cooked chili has been cooled, skim off the saturated fat from the surface; then stir in a small amount of extra virgin olive oil. I recommend preparing chili at least a day in advance, so the saturated fat can be skimmed off and to give the flavor time to mature.

4. All the ingredients should be as fresh as possible to obtain the best results. Spicing is given in average amounts in these chili recipes; since tastes will vary, this should be personally adjusted. Also, the strength of spices varies with their freshness.

5. The meat used in making chili can vary. Beef, chicken, veal and turkey will all produce great chili. And any type of cut can be used. Since the chili simmers for many hours, a tougher cut is suitable as well as ground meat.

6. If beans are part of the chili, use precooked ones and add them only when the chili has finished cooking. If they are added too soon, they will overcook and turn to mush.

Chili can be served in many different ways. It is hearty enough to stand alone in a bowl as a meal or snack. It can be served over rice, any type of pasta, or any cooked grain. Try plain cooked buckwheat (kasha), bulgar or millet. Chili is great on a hamburger (with or without the bun)! And it can be a great side dish, or it can sauce up plain steamed chicken or roast. Or serve chili over fresh steamed vegetables.

Veal Chili

Serve this over a bed of rice (brown or white), kasha or pasta. As an option you may add 2 tbsp (25 mL) extra virgin olive oil after fat is skimmed.

2 to 2½ lb	boneless stewing veal, cut in ½-inch (1 cm) cubes	1 to 1.25 kg
4 tbsp	all-purpose flour	50 mL
1½ tsp	Season All	7 mL
1	onion, chopped	1
1	can (5½ oz/156 mL) tomato paste	1
2 cups	water	500 mL
½ cup	tequila (optional)	125 mL
3	large cloves garlic, chopped	3
½ tsp	freshly ground pepper	2 mL
3 tbsp	Worcestershire sauce	50 mL
3 tbsp	(approx) hot pepper sauce (less or more to taste)	50 mL
4 to 5 tbsp	chili powder	50 to 75 mL

Wash veal cubes and remove any fat; sprinkle veal with flour and Season All. In dry non-stick skillet, sauté veal until browned. Remove veal to large pot. In same skillet, sauté onion until lightly browned; add to veal.

In large measuring cup or bowl, mix remaining ingredients. Add to pot of veal; stir well. Cook, uncovered, over low heat for 2 hours. Check sauce from time to time: it should reduce and thicken. (If it reduces too much, it is cooking too rapidly. Reduce heat and add a little water to correct.) Near the end of cooking time, taste and adjust spices.

Refrigerate overnight. Skim fat from surface. Reheat gently before serving.

Veal Chili with Vegetables
To the basic recipe, add the following to the sauce 10 minutes before chili is fully cooked: 2 large carrots, chopped; 2 stalks celery, finely chopped; 1 cup (250 mL) thickly sliced mushrooms.

Chili with Beans

2 to 2½ lb	lean or extra-lean ground beef or chunks of lean stewing beef	1 to 1.25 kg
¼ cup	all-purpose flour	50 mL
1½ tsp	Season All	7 mL
½ tsp	freshly ground pepper	2 mL
1	onion, chopped	1
3	large cloves garlic, minced	3
1	can (5½ oz/156 mL) tomato paste	1
2 cups	water	500 mL
1 cup	light beer	250 mL
3 tbsp	Dijon mustard	50 mL
1 to 2 tbsp	hot pepper sauce	15 to 25 mL
½ cup	strong black coffee	125 mL
4 to 5 tbsp	chili powder	50 to 75 mL
1	can (19 oz/540 mL) red kidney beans	1

In dry non-stick pan, place beef. Sprinkle with flour, Season All and pepper. Brown meat; transfer to a large pot. Brown onion and garlic; add to meat. Mix tomato paste into water; add to meat.

Turn heat under meat pot to medium; when mixture starts to cook, reduce heat to low. Add remaining ingredients except beans. Simmer, uncovered, for 2 hours. Occasionally check the moisture level; add water if required. Near the end of cooking time, taste and adjust spices. Remove from heat and stir in beans.

Refrigerate overnight. Skim fat from surface. Reheat gently before serving.

Variation:
Add 1 tbsp (15 mL) extra virgin olive oil after the fat is skimmed.

Chili Mac

This dish is quickly becoming popular across the country. Next time a large pot of chili (any type) is cooking, cook some elbow macaroni until al dente. Drain well. Amounts do not have to be exact, but use approximately 2 cups (500 mL) cooked macaroni to 1½ cups (375 mL) chili. Mix macaroni into chili. Serve immediately, or place in serving-size microwave-safe containers and freeze for fast snacks or lunches and dinners on the run.

If a family meal is being planned, fill a large casserole with Chili Mac. Sprinkle with ¼ cup (50 mL) shredded extra-old low-fat Cheddar cheese or grated Parmesan. Bake in 350°F (180°C) oven for 15 to 20 minutes until casserole is hot and cheese is browned. Serve with a fresh garden salad.

Vegetarian Chili

Serve this hot over pasta or cooked grains. It also makes a great sauce for meat or poultry. Or serve it in a bowl sprinkled with extra-old low-fat Cheddar cheese.

1 tbsp	virgin olive oil	15 mL
1	large onion, coarsely chopped	1
3	large cloves garlic, minced	3
1	green bell pepper, chopped	1
1	stalk celery, finely chopped	1
1	can (5½ oz/156 mL) tomato paste	1
2 cups	water	500 mL
3	carrots, cut in rounds	3
3	tomatoes, peeled, seeded and coarsely chopped	3
3 tbsp	Worcestershire sauce	50 mL
1 to 3 tbsp	hot pepper sauce	15 to 50 mL
4 to 5 tbsp	chili powder	50 to 75 mL
1 cup	thickly sliced mushrooms	250 mL
1 cup	frozen corn kernels	250 mL
1	can (19 oz/540 mL) red kidney beans, drained	1

In skillet, heat oil; sauté onion and garlic until browned. Transfer to large pot. In same skillet, sauté green pepper and celery until softened; add to large pot. Mix tomato paste with water; add to pot. Start to simmer over low heat. Stir in carrots, tomatoes, Worcestershire sauce, hot pepper sauce and chili powder. Simmer, uncovered, on low heat for 15 minutes. Add mushrooms, corn and kidney beans. Taste and adjust spices. Cook, uncovered, for a further 15 minutes. Add 2 tbsp (25 mL) extra virgin olive oil after cooking, if desired.

Updated Beef and Veal

Roast Beef

The types of cuts available will vary depending on what is popular in your local area. The spicing and cooking variations described here can be used for any cut or style of roast beef. For those who want a very lean roast, I recommend a cut called point brisket. Point brisket comes in two styles — a whole brisket that has a small section of fat, marbled meat, and a single brisket that has had the fatty part removed.

I have seen this rather large and flat cut of meat sold in strange ways. Some meat retailers have been cutting it down the middle, rolling it and tying it. If it comes that way, untie the roast, spice it and cook it flat. Roasting it flat will not dry out this great cut of meat. (Have a talk with your butcher about not butchering this beautiful roast.)

Whichever type of roast you choose, these methods of cooking and spicing will give you a moist, delicious roast. The point brisket is the cut that is used to make corned beef, pastrami and smoked beef. The brisket is also available in veal; however, that cut is harder to find. Take note that the veal brisket is not available in the large sizes of beef brisket, due to the size of the animal.

Roasted Beef

Start with any favorite cut of roast beef. Rinse the beef under cold water, and remove any visible excess fat. Place the roast into the roasting pan and spice it on all sides. If it is possible to refrigerate the spiced roast overnight or even 2 or 3 hours before cooking, this will enhance the flavor. However, it is not essential — the roast may be cooked as soon as it is spiced.

It is not necessary to defrost a roast before cooking, but the cooking time must be adjusted accordingly. If you like roast beef with a rare center and well done on the outside, start with a frozen roast. The freezing will slow down the cooking in the center.

The amount of spice used in these recipes can vary according to personal taste and the size of the roast. The amounts given here are a guideline, and are given for one side of the roast; spicing should be repeated on the other side.

When cooking any roast with little or no fat, it is best to place about ½ to 1 cup (125 mL to 250 mL) liquid in the pan. This can be water; half water, half wine (white or red); or beer. Cover the roast for most or all of the cooking time. If the roast is to be well done, do not uncover it. Shorter cooking times for a rare roast will require some browning with the cover off, about 15 minutes before the roast is removed from the oven.

Brisket is one of those roasts that needs to be well cooked, but not overcooked or it will be too dry. Roasting can be done slowly at 325°F (160°C) or at 350°F (180°C). Approximate timing will be about 20 minutes per pound (500 g) at 350°F (180°C), 30 minutes per pound (500 g) at 325°F (160°C). Check for tenderness with a fork.

Tip:
For those who use kosher meats, part of the koshering process is salting of the meat, which can add two to three times more sodium to the meat compared with its "unkoshered" counterpart. Soaking koshered beef or veal in cold water for an hour can remove much of the excess sodium. Rinse well; then cook.

Spicing Combination #1 (for one side of the roast)

1 to 2 tbsp	Dijon mustard	15 to 25 mL
1 tbsp	granulated garlic	15 mL
1 tbsp	granulated onion	15 mL
1 tbsp	green peppercorns, crushed	15 mL
2 tsp	chili powder	10 mL
2 tsp	Season All (optional)	10 mL

Rub mustard into meat. Sprinkle with remaining spices in the order given. Turn over roast; repeat on other side.

½ cup	dry red or white wine	125 mL
½ cup	water	125 mL

Combine wine with water. Pour around meat in roasting pan. Roast meat, covered, in 325°F (160°C) oven for 30 minutes per pound (500 g); check roast after 1 to 1½ hours. About 15 minutes before roast is done, raise heat to 350°F (180°C) and remove cover to allow meat to brown.

Spicing Combination #2 (for one side of the roast)

3	large cloves of garlic, chopped	3
¼ cup	prepared mustard	50 mL
2 tbsp	Worcestershire sauce	25 mL
1 tbsp	dried tarragon	15 mL
1 tbsp	granulated onion	15 mL
1 tsp	freshly ground pepper	5 mL

Mix all ingredients into a paste; coat one side of roast. Turn over roast and repeat. Refrigerate for 2 to 3 hours or overnight.

¾ to 1 cup	dry red wine	175 to 250 mL

Pour wine around meat in roasting pan. Proceed as in Spicing Combination #1.

Spicing Combination #3 (for one side of the roast)

1 tbsp	Worcestershire sauce	15 mL
2 tsp	granulated garlic	10 mL
2 tsp	granulated onion	10 mL
1 tbsp	Season All	15 mL
1 tbsp	whole black peppercorns, roughly crushed	15 mL
4 tbsp	whole pickling spice, roughly crushed	50 mL

Rub Worcestershire sauce into one side of meat. Spice that side with everything except pickling spice. Turn meat over; repeat. Press 2 tbsp (25 mL) pickling spice into bottom of roast; place roast in roasting pan. Press 2 tbsp (25 mL) pickling spice into top of roast.

½ cup	dry wine or light beer	125 mL
½ cup	water	125 mL

Combine wine with water; pour around meat in roasting pan. Proceed as in Spicing Combination #1.

Notes:
Buy four pepper mills. Fill one with black peppercorns; another with green peppercorns; the third with white peppercorns; and the fourth with pickling spice. These are handy for all types of cooking, not just beef. A sprinkle of any of these will add so much to the flavor. Use the pickling spice along with any of the peppercorns.

A very handy item every kitchen should have is a fat-removal broom, which allows you to remove the fat from the surface of anything without refrigerating. Another handy way to do this is with a special measuring cup with a lowered spout. This allows the gravy in the lower part to be poured out while the fat on top remains in the measuring cup. Both items can be found in kitchen or department stores.

Texas Oven-Baked Barbecue Beef

This is a terrific recipe to use on a tougher cut of meat, though any cut will work really well. Go for a roast with little or no fat. Brisket works well, as do round and rump roast. This beef requires a long cooking time, but is simple to make. It can be precooked the day before. If there are any leftovers, they freeze well. Several roasts can be made to feed a large group.

3 lb	(minimum) roast	1.5 kg
1 tbsp	granulated onion	15 mL
1 tbsp	granulated garlic	15 mL
1 tbsp	Season All	15 mL
½ tsp	freshly ground black pepper	2 mL
½ cup	dry red or white wine	125 mL
½ tsp	liquid smoke (optional)	2 mL
1 to 2 cups	Barbecue Sauce (pg. 64)	250 to 500 mL

Rinse roast in cold water; trim off any visible fat. For each 3 lb (1.5 kg) meat, spice roast on all sides with given amounts of onion, garlic, Season All and pepper.

Place roast in roasting pan. Combine wine with liquid smoke (if using); pour into pan. Cover roaster with aluminum foil (shiny side up); cook in 325°F (160°C) oven for 30 minutes per pound (500 kg). Because of second roasting to come, meat can be slightly underdone at this stage.

Remove roast from oven. Place meat on slicing board. Using sharp knife, cut into rough slices (large slices of meat can be sliced into 3 or 4 sections, or rip strips of meat from the roast until it is all in shredded pieces).

Drain all drippings from pan; reserve. Return cut meat to pan. Pour over meat: Barbecue Sauce or Hickory-Smoked Barbecue Sauce (pg. 64) mixed with ¾ cup (175 mL) of the fat-skimmed pan juices. (The amount of sauce required will depend on the amount of meat. Meat should be well coated.) Return meat, covered, to 350°F (180°C) oven for 20 to 30 minutes (depending on how well cooked the roast was during the first roasting).

Beef Stew with Extras

This stew starts with beef, but the great flavor comes from the variety of other meats that go into it. The vegetables and meats can vary, according to what may be available and your own favorites.

¾ to 1 lb	stewing beef or stewing veal (or combination), all visible fat removed	375 to 500 g
	Granulated onion	
	Granulated garlic	
	Season All	
	All-purpose flour	
4	chicken legs or thighs, skin and all visible fat removed	4
5 cups	water	1.25 L
2 tbsp	low-sodium chicken soup powder	25 mL
2 tbsp	low-sodium beef soup powder	25 mL
4 tsp	dried tarragon	20 mL
1 tsp	freshly ground black pepper	5 mL
½ tsp	dried sage	2 mL
¼ cup	Scotch or dry white wine (optional)	50 mL
1	onion, cut in 8 wedges	1
3	carrots, peeled and cut into chunks	3
3	potatoes, peeled and cut into 2-inch (5 cm) chunks	3
1 cup	green beans, cut into 2-inch (5 cm) pieces (or snow peas or frozen green peas added just before stew is done)	250 mL
1 cup	small whole mushrooms	250 mL
1 cup	zucchini, cut into 1-inch (7 cm) chunks	250 mL
3 tbsp	all-purpose flour	50 mL
1 cup	water	250 mL

10   (approx) frozen cooked   10
         meatballs
         (if you have some in
         freezer; if not, add extra
         chicken, beef or veal)

Wash stewing beef with cold water. Cut into 2-inch (5 cm) chunks. Spice with onion, garlic and Season All; dust with flour. Brown in non-stick pan coated with olive oil spray. When meat is browned, place it in large pot.

Spice and flour chicken as with beef. Brown in pan with olive oil spray. When browned, add to beef. Reserve pan.

Pour water into pot of browned meat. Turn heat to high; when water starts to boil, reduce heat to medium. Add chicken soup powder, beef soup powder, tarragon, black pepper, sage and Scotch (if using).

In pan that meat was cooked in, brown onion. Add to the stewing meat.

Add carrots; cook over medium-low heat, partially covered, for 15 minutes. Add potatoes; cook for 10 minutes. Add green beans; cook for 10 minutes. Add mushrooms, zucchini and peas (if using). Cook for 5 to 7 minutes. Dissolve flour in water; add to gravy. Cook to thicken, about 2 minutes. Makes 6 to 8 servings.

Fire Steak #1

This can easily be made using a lean whole eye of the round roast. The fillet can be bought several days before using, to let the spices blend, or once the spices have blended, it can be frozen for later use. This Fire Steak can be made two ways, whole as a Fire Steak Roast or cut into steaks 1½ to 2 inches (4 cm to 5 cm) thick.

1	whole eye of the round roast (sized to your needs)	1
⅓ cup	whole black peppercorns	75 mL
2 tbsp	whole pickling spices	25 mL
1 tbsp	granulated onion	15 mL
1 tbsp	granulated garlic	15 mL

Place peppercorns and pickling spices in a small plastic bag; roll with rolling pin to crush. Place crushed peppercorns, pickling spices, onion and garlic on piece of waxed paper. Mix well.

   Wash roast; pat damp dry with paper towel. Roll meat in peppercorn mixture to coat; press well into meat. If the roast is very large, it may be necessary to double amount of spices to properly coat meat.

   Wrap roast in waxed paper; place in plastic bag. Seal well and refrigerate for at least 24 hours.

   Barbecue or broil steaks. As a roast, slice as desired.

Fire Steak #2

This Fire Steak is a bit different. It is quite economical, fantastic looking and great tasting.

• For each fire steak, prepare ¼ lb (125 g) extra-lean ground beef, chicken, veal, turkey or combinations, and a quantity of pan-fry thin-cut round steak.

⅓ cup	whole black peppercorns	75 mL
2 tbsp	whole pickling spice	25 mL
1 tbsp	granulated garlic	15 mL
1 tbsp	granulated onion	15 mL

Mix 3 to 4 lb (1.5 kg to 2 kg) ground meat. (These steaks freeze well and are ready to barbecue or broil at any time, so make extra.) Use recipe for Better-than-Ever Hamburger (pg. 99).

Wash thin round steak slices with cold water. Pat dry with paper towel. Using sharp knife, slice the round steak in long strips about 1½ to 2 inches (4 cm to 5 cm) wide.

Form about ¼ lb (125 g) ground meat into fat hamburger, 1½ to 2 inches (4 cm to 5 cm) thick. Wrap a round steak strip around the outside edge of the meat; the ends should overlap about 1 to 1½ inches (2.5 cm to 4 cm). Secure round steak strip with toothpick.

Using the palm of your hand, press down gently on ground meat to form a bond to the round steak. Complete remainder of steaks.

Place peppercorns and pickling spice in plastic bag; use rolling pin to crush. Mix with garlic and onion. Place on sheet of waxed paper. Roll round steak side of each Fire Steak in peppercorn mixture. (If freezing, wrap each steak separately in waxed paper; freeze in tightly closed freezer bag.)

Barbecue, broil or pan-fry in a dry non-stick pan. The taste can be varied by changing the combinations of ground meat.

Note:
A rare steak can be achieved by cooking frozen meat. This way the outside can be charred and crisp, while the inside remains rare or medium-rare.

Veal Parmigiana

This classic Italian dish can be made with any cut of veal, but ground extra-lean white veal works well and is more economical. The meat can be prepared, made into patties and frozen for quick assembly and baking. Wrap each patty in waxed paper; freeze in a plastic bag.

1½ lbs	extra-lean ground veal or combined with chicken	750 g
1	egg (or 2 egg whites)	1
3 tbsp	Worcestershire sauce	50 mL
3 tbsp	prepared mustard	50 mL
3 tbsp	ketchup	50 mL
½ cup	bread crumbs	125 mL
¼ cup	(approx) water	50 mL
2 tsp	each granulated onion, granulated garlic, chili powder	10 mL
1 tbsp	mixed Italian herbs	15 mL
1	can (28 oz/796 mL) tomato sauce (no-salt)	1
3 tbsp	mixed Italian herbs	50 mL
1 tbsp	each granulated garlic, granulated onion, chili powder	15 mL
3 tbsp	grated Parmesan cheese	50 mL
6 tbsp	shredded skim-milk mozzarella cheese	90 mL

Mix together well meat, egg, Worcestershire sauce, mustard, ketchup, bread crumbs, water, 2 tsp (10 mL) each onion, garlic and chili, and 1 tbsp (15 mL) Italian spices. Add more water if necessary. Form into 6 patties. Place patties in glass baking dish.

Blend together tomato sauce, 3 tbsp (50 mL) Italian herbs, and 1 tbsp (15 mL) each garlic, onion and chili. Pour sauce over patties. Sprinkle with Parmesan cheese. Cover with foil. Bake in 350°F (180°C) oven for 20 to 25 minutes if meat is fresh, 25 to 35 minutes if frozen. Remove from oven; remove cover; and sprinkle each patty with 1 tbsp (15 mL) mozzarella cheese. Return to oven with heat turned off. Leave for 2 to 4 minutes just to melt cheese. Makes 6 patties.

Veal Marsala

This is a very fast and simple dish. It works equally well with slices of a turkey or chicken breast that have been pounded thin.

1 to 2	thin slices veal per person	1 to 2
	Granulated onion	
	Granulated garlic	
	Season All	
	Freshly ground green peppercorns	
	All-purpose flour	
½ lb	sliced mushrooms	250 g
1 tbsp	lemon juice	15 mL
½ cup	dry white wine	125 mL

Sprinkle each side of veal with granulated onion, granulated garlic, Season All and green peppercorns. Dust lightly with flour.

In large non-stick skillet with olive oil spray, brown veal on one side; turn to other side. Add mushrooms and lemon juice. Let meat brown. Add wine. Reduce wine for about 5 minutes. Serve immediately.

Stove-top Beef Chunks Simmered in Wine

This fast and easy meal can be prepared with beef or veal chunks. Serve with plain steamed rice, a rice and bean combination, noodles, buckwheat or bulgar. Lots of steamed vegetables will complete this hearty meal.

2 lb	stewing beef chunks, fat removed	1 kg
	Flour (for dredging)	
1 tbsp	virgin olive oil	15 mL
1	large onion, thinly sliced	1
7	large cloves garlic, sliced	7
1/4 tsp	freshly ground black pepper	1 mL
1/4 tsp	dried sage	1 mL
2 tsp	Season All	10 mL
1/2 cup	dry red or white wine	125 mL
5	frozen beef soup cubes (or 1/2 cup/125 mL water with 1 1/2 tsp/7 mL low-sodium beef soup powder)	5
1 1/2 tsp	all-purpose flour	7 mL
1/4 cup	water	50 mL
1 cup	thickly sliced mushrooms	250 mL

Wash beef; pat dry. Lightly coat with flour.

In skillet, heat olive oil. Sauté onion and garlic for a few seconds; add beef. Sprinkle pepper, sage and Season All over meat while browning. Meat should be well browned, but do not let onion and garlic burn.

When meat has browned, add wine and soup cubes. Simmer over medium heat for 12 to 14 minutes. If liquid cooks down too low, add water. Dissolve flour in 1/4 cup (50 mL) water; add to meat when chunks are just about ready. Add mushrooms during the last 2 to 3 minutes of cooking. Check meat for doneness with a fork; it should be quite tender. Makes 4 servings.

Marvelous Chicken

Chicken

This wonderful versatile food has found a new place in our regular diet. It is no wonder, because it is a protein that is easy to digest and can be prepared without fat. For a long time, chicken breasts have been a staple on low-calorie diets.

The chicken recipes in this book require that all skin and visible fat be removed before cooking. Most of the chicken that I prepare for my family is done with chicken breasts only, but in some of the recipes I have indicated that other parts may be used equally well.

When you buy chicken breasts, look for plump, large, well-rounded ones. If the chicken has an odor, it is not fresh. Breasts can be bought with the skin, fat and bone already removed — handy when time is short. I recommend that if you have the time, buy the breasts whole and fresh, and remove the fat and skin yourself. It's cheaper. The bone can be removed or remain in. I like to freeze the bones and cook a large pot of them into a Basic Chicken Soup (pg. 40).

The skin can be removed from every part of the chicken except the flat part of the wing and the tip. The wing of the chicken should not be used if cholesterol and calories are to be limited in your diet.

After removing skin and fat, place chicken in a large bowl and sprinkle it with salt. Pour enough boiling water over the chicken to submerge it. Let chicken sit in the bath for a few minutes before pouring off the water. Rinse the chicken well in cool water; drain off excess water. The chicken is now ready to use or package for the freezer. The skin will be easier to remove from a whole chicken after it has this bath, and the possibility of harmful bacteria remaining alive is no longer a problem. *Note*: If you are on a sodium-controlled diet, use a potassium salt substitute instead of the salt in the bath. Lemon juice can also substitute for the salt.

Boneless breasts have the advantage of being on my fast-food list, since they require little fuss and little time to prepare. They can be cooked with a whole range of spices, herbs, sauces and vegetables.

I recommend cleaning and preparing the chicken when your schedule will permit. At that time, a large quantity can be cleaned, packaged and frozen in the amounts you will need. Breasts can be packaged individually by wrapping each in waxed paper and placing a quantity in a freezer bag. Remove as many as needed for each meal.

Skinning and Boning a Whole Chicken Breast

1. After rinsing the breasts in cold water, place a half breast on a work surface, skin side up. (Never use a wooden chopping surface for any type of food preparation, as it can never be cleaned thoroughly enough to remove all the bacteria that live deep in the pores of the wood.) Peel away the skin starting at an edge. Using a very sharp knife, trim away any remaining bits of skin or fat.

2. Insert the tip of a very sharp knife (not a large one) under the flesh at the rib side of the breast. Keeping the knife as close as possible to the ribs, work the knife toward the breastbone. After reaching the breastbone, turn the breast over to the other side and repeat with the other half of the breast.

3. With the sharp knife, scrape the meat away from the breastbone on both sides. Loosen the wishbone with the sharp knife. Being careful not to tear the meat, gently pull any attached part away from the breastbone.

Tip:
To flatten a chicken breast, place it between two sheets of waxed paper; using a mallet or the bottom of a drinking glass, pound gently with light, even strokes until meat is the desired thinness.

The Tenderest Chicken Breasts
To assure the most tender and sweet-tasting chicken no
matter how it is prepared, place fatless, skinless, deboned and
lightly pounded chicken breasts into a bath of 2 tbsp (25 mL)
cornstarch per 1 cup (250 mL) cold water. All the chicken
should be immersed. Cover and refrigerate for 2 hours or
more. Rinse the breasts in cold water. Dry, and wrap for
freezing or use fresh in any recipe.

Chicken breasts that remain on the bone but that have had
all skin and fat removed may also be soaked this way.

Italian Parmesan Chicken

With the chicken breasts cleaned and deboned before
preparation, this is a fast stove-to-table meal after a long day.
Served with steamed vegetables and brown rice, it makes a
great dinner.

Allow 1 half breast or more per person, depending on the
size of the breasts.

4 to 6	half chicken breasts, skinned and deboned	4 to 6
⅓ cup	tomato paste (no salt or sugar)	75 mL
½ cup	dry white wine	125 mL
½ cup	water	125 mL
1 tbsp	virgin olive oil	15 mL
1	onion, chopped	1
6 to 8	cloves garlic, sliced	6 to 8
1	tomato, chopped	1
½ tsp	white pepper	2 mL
1½ tsp	chili powder	7 mL
1 tbsp	Italian herbs	15 mL
1½ tsp	dried tarragon	7 mL
4 or 5	large mushrooms, thickly sliced	4 or 5
2 to 3 tbsp	grated Parmesan cheese	25 to 50 mL

In bowl, blend tomato paste with wine and water. Set aside. In large skillet coated with olive oil, sauté onion and garlic; when they begin to brown, add tomato and tomato paste mixture.

Stir into pan pepper, chili powder, Italian herbs and tarragon. When sauce is hot, add chicken. Cook over medium heat for 5 minutes. Turn breasts. Add mushrooms; cook for 5 minutes. Turn breasts; sprinkle with Parmesan. Cook until breasts feel firm and sauce has thickened. Makes 4 to 6 servings.

Creamed Corn Chicken

I usually make this with chicken breasts, but other parts of the chicken may be used as long as the skin and visible fat have been removed. Use 1 chicken breast half per person, or proportionate amounts of other parts.

5 to 6	half chicken breasts	5 to 6
1½ cups	frozen corn, thawed	375 mL
4	cloves garlic	4
⅓ cup	water	75 mL
⅓ cup	instant skim-milk powder	75 mL
½ cup	water	125 mL
1 tbsp	low-sodium chicken soup powder	15 mL
2 tbsp	low-sodium soy sauce	25 mL
2 tbsp	white wine	25 mL
1 tbsp	sesame seed oil	15 mL
Pinch	ground ginger	Pinch
¼ tsp	white pepper	1 mL
2	green onions, chopped	2
2 tbsp	cornstarch	25 mL

In food processor or blender, using on/off pulsating action, process corn, garlic, ⅓ cup (75 mL) water and skim-milk powder until corn is chopped but mixture is not puréed.

Pour corn mixture into a bowl. Mix ½ cup (125 mL) water and chicken soup powder; add to corn. Stir in soy sauce, wine, sesame seed oil, ginger, pepper, green onions and cornstarch.

Place chicken into glass baking dish large enough to hold it all in a single layer. Pour creamed corn mixture over chicken; cover with foil. Bake in a 350°F (180°C) oven for 40 to 45 minutes or until fork-tender. Makes 5 to 6 servings.

Chicken Fingers

These are great for a fast meal when you plan ahead. Make these in quantity and freeze them for a heat-and-eat dinner. If the chicken is cut into nuggets, they make great appetizers. Try your favorite dipping sauce (or Barbecue Sauce, pg. 64).

Allow between ½ and 1 whole chicken breast per person, depending on the size of the breasts and the appetites. Leftovers can be easily reheated.

4	whole chicken breasts, deboned, skinned and fat removed	4
1 cup	dry bread crumbs	250 mL
2 tsp	granulated onion	10 mL
2 tsp	granulated garlic	10 mL
2 tsp	Season All	10 mL
3 tbsp	grated Parmesan cheese	50 mL
¼ tsp	freshly ground pepper	1 mL
1	egg white	1
2 tbsp	water	25 mL

In a large flat dish, combine bread crumbs, onion, garlic, Season All, Parmesan and pepper. Beat egg white with water.

Cut chicken breasts lengthwise into strips about ½ inch (1 cm) wide.

Heat large non-stick skillet coated with vegetable spray. (If calories and fat are not a concern, 1 to 2 tbsp/15 mL to 25 mL canola oil may be used.)

Dunk chicken strips in egg; coat well with bread crumb mixture. Brown chicken strips in skillet. Chicken strips may be eaten hot or cold. Serves 4 to 5.

Variation:
Half breasts can also be done the same way without cutting them into fingers. Serve breasts with sauce or a wedge of lemon.

Barbecued Chicken

Aside from being a great chicken dish, this is very easy and adapts well for large groups.

Allow 2 or 3 small chicken pieces per person or 1 or 2 large chicken pieces per person.

Remove the heavily fat-laden parts of the skin and all visible chunks of fat. Small amounts of lean skin may remain. Follow the procedures for cleaning the chicken (pg. 125).

Before the chicken is placed on a grill, it must be partially cooked. The uneven size and shape of chicken parts would require an extended time on the grill to cook the thicker parts, and a lot of burned and dried-out chicken would result.

Par-cooking the chicken can be done in several ways. The fastest and easiest is in the microwave oven. Follow the microwave directions with your oven to partially cook the chicken.

The chicken can be oven-steamed for a short time by placing it in a roaster, pouring in 1½ cups (375 mL) water, covering tightly and steaming in 350°F (180°C) oven for 20 to 30 minutes.

Remove the partially cooked chicken to a large platter; sprinkle each piece of chicken with granulated garlic. At this point, the chicken can be refrigerated for barbecuing at a later time that day or the next.

Place chicken on the grill about 4 inches (10 cm) above hot coals. After each side has had one turn on the grill, brush barbecue sauce on each side. Watch the chicken so it does not burn. It will not take long to finish cooking.

Serve extra sauce on the side.

Variation:
This chicken can also be cooked in the oven. After the chicken is partially cooked using the oven-steaming method, remove from oven, drain away water and sprinkle with granulated garlic. Brush chicken with barbecue sauce; return chicken, uncovered, to the oven. Bake at 350°F (180°C) for 20 minutes; remove and brush with a thick coating of sauce; return to oven, cooking until fork-tender. Serve extra sauce on the side.

Skinny Shake and Bake

This is my trimmed-down version of an old family favorite. You may use any combination of chicken parts in whatever quantity you want, so long as all skin and visible fat are removed.

1	whole chicken (skin and fat removed), cut into 6 to 8 pieces	1
½ cup	crushed cornflakes	125 mL
2 tsp	granulated garlic	10 mL
2 tsp	granulated onion	10 mL
2 tsp	Season All	10 mL
2 tsp	chili powder	10 mL
1 tbsp	grated Parmesan cheese	15 mL

Wash and drain chicken.

In a strong clean plastic bag, place (for each 6 to 8 chicken pieces): cornflakes, garlic, onion, Season All, chili powder and Parmesan. Hold bag closed; shake to mix well. Place 1 piece of chicken at a time into bag; shake well to coat.

Place chicken parts in shallow roasting pan or large glass baking dish. Add ¼ inch (5 mm) water. Cover pan with foil wrap, shiny side up. Bake in 350°F (180°C) oven for 45 to 60 minutes, removing cover in last 10 minutes of baking.

Chicken Breasts with Tarragon and White Wine

Remember to remove all skin and fat. Serve with pasta and steamed vegetables.

4	large half chicken breasts	4
1 tbsp	virgin olive oil	15 mL
½ cup	chopped green onions	125 mL
2 tbsp	chopped fresh tarragon (or 2 tsp/10 mL dried)	25 mL
	Freshly ground black pepper	
½ cup	dry white wine	125 mL
¼ cup	chicken stock (or 1 tsp/5 mL low-sodium chicken soup powder dissolved in ¼ cup/50 mL water)	50 mL

In pan over medium-high heat, sauté chicken in olive oil for 2 to 3 minutes on each side or until lightly browned.

Reduce heat to medium. Add green onions, tarragon, pepper, wine and chicken stock. Cook, covered, for 8 minutes. Uncover; cook for 2 minutes until tender. (Timing may be different for other parts of the chicken. Always check for doneness.) Remove chicken to heated platter. Pour sauce from pan over chicken. Makes 4 servings.

How to Make Great Turkey

If possible, use a fresh turkey. If this cannot be obtained, buy
a frozen turkey and allow two days for thawing. If possible,
avoid the type that is injected with oil or butter. If not, this
oil can be easily removed in the cleaning process. The turkey
will be moist and taste great when the following procedures
are followed.

If a fresh bird is being used, start with directions for Day
Three.

Days One and Two
Thaw the turkey in the refrigerator for 2 days.

Day Three (Preparation)
Remove the bird from the refrigerator. Remove all the
wrapping; place the turkey in a clean sink. Pour salt over the
bird and into the cavity. Let turkey sit. Meanwhile, boil a
large pot of water. Pour the boiling water over turkey and
into cavity.

Clean out the inside, pulling away any fat or other debris.
Check the outside and remove any large globs of fat around
the neck. The neck, if still attached, can be removed.

Rinse the turkey inside and out with lots of cool water.

Place the turkey, breast side down, in a roasting pan.
Sprinkle over the bird the following spices. The amounts will
depend on the size of the turkey. The amounts given work
for a 5- to 12-kg (11- to 26-lb) turkey.

2 to 3 tbsp	granulated garlic	25 to 50 mL
2 to 3 tbsp	granulated onion	25 to 50 mL
2 to 3 tbsp	Season All	25 to 50 mL
1 tbsp	freshly ground white pepper	15 mL
1 tbsp	chili powder	15 mL

Turn the turkey over and repeat the spicing. Cover the bird
with foil; place in the refrigerator until the following day. (If
standing time is not available, the turkey can be cooked at
once.)

Day Four (Cooking)

Remove the turkey from the refrigerator; pour into the roasting pan 1 cup (250 mL) dry white wine. Extra water may be added to the pan during cooking.

Arrange the turkey breast side down. Cover tightly with foil (shiny side up), and place it into a 350°F (180°C) oven. Unstuffed turkey should take about 20 minutes per pound (500 g).

About 30 minutes before cooking is completed, remove foil; turn turkey breast side up. Roast for another 20 to 30 minutes until the turkey is golden. Test for doneness by moving a drumstick; if it moves easily, meat is done. The meat will also shrink away from the end of the drumstick.

Remove the turkey from the oven; let stand about 15 minutes. Pour off all the gravy into a container; refrigerate to allow the fat to solidify. Turkey may be: re-covered with foil and refrigerated until the next day, as it cuts better when cold; or carved if it is allowed to cool for about 45 minutes, then reheated just before serving.

Day of Serving

Remove the turkey from the refrigerator, and sharpen a good carving knife. Place the bird on a carving board. Remove and discard all skin.

Start by removing the legs. Slice off the meat and place in a clean roasting pan lined with foil. Proceed with the dark meat of the turkey, placing the slices in the roasting pan. (A microwave dish can substitute if that is where the turkey will be warmed.)

Slice the white meat evenly and thinly. Layer the white meat beside the dark meat. The wings can be separated into two pieces each, and kept intact.

Remove and discard all the fat from the top of the gravy container; pour the remaining gravy into a saucepan large enough to hold twice its quantity. Estimate the quantity of gravy, and measure out 1 level tbsp (15 mL) flour per cup (250 mL) gravy. Place the flour into a measuring cup; add 1 cup (250 mL) water, stirring until flour is blended and smooth. Start to heat the gravy. Pour the flour mixture into the gravy; let it start cooking. Add about 1 cup (250 mL) of additional water to thin the gravy to the desired consistency. Check the spicing; more may be added to taste.

Refrigerate the turkey and gravy until time to heat. Sprinkle a small amount of water over meat before heating in the oven or the microwave. Keep meat well covered while heating to prevent drying. Remove to a platter or serve directly from the microwave dish.

Turkey in Beer

This recipe is not just limited to whole turkey, because turkey parts are now becoming available. This makes a terrific bird for any occasion.

1	whole turkey	1
1 tbsp	chili powder	15 mL
1 to 2 tbsp	granulated onion	15 to 25 mL
1 to 2 tbsp	granulated garlic	15 to 25 mL
1 to 2 tbsp	Season All	15 to 25 mL
1 tbsp	freshly ground black pepper	15 mL
1 can	light beer	1

Clean turkey. Remove excess fat globs and fatty skin. The rest of the skin may be left on for roasting. Sprinkle chili powder, onion, garlic, Season All and pepper all over turkey. Place bird breast side down in roasting pan.

Pour beer into roaster. Cover turkey with foil; roast in 350°F (180°C) oven for 20 minutes per pound (500 g). Remove foil in the last 30 minutes of cooking; turn turkey breast side up. Test for doneness (move a drumstick; if it moves easily, meat is done).

When turkey is done, let stand for 15 to 20 minutes before carving. The juices in the pan make terrific gravy.

Note:
A whole turkey can be done by spicing, refrigerating, then cooking the day before, and carving cold the day of serving. Follow the directions in "How to Make Great Turkey" (pg. 133). I do not recommend cooking turkey in a paper bag, as we now cannot be sure what chemicals are used in the manufacture of those bags.

Variation:
Use half or whole turkey breast. Clean and remove any fat and skin. Place breast in roasting pan; pour can of light beer over breast. Spice; cover with lid or foil. Bake in 350°F (180°C) oven for about 1 hour, depending on size. Test for doneness with a fork. Skim fat from the liquid and make great gravy from the drippings. Any of your favorite turkey parts can be done this way for a great turkey dinner anytime, or when there are only 1 or 2 people and a whole turkey is too much. A half turkey breast, depending on the size, will serve 4 to 5 people. Adjust spices accordingly.

The turkey will pick up flavors from whatever it is cooked with; do not hesitate to try new things. Fruits such as apples, grapes, peaches, oranges and grapefruit may be added to the pan with the turkey. These fruits will give the turkey a subtle but new taste. Wine or beer will accompany the use of fruit very well.

Chicken Broccoli Roll-Ups

This is a very impressive-looking dish, and it is fast and easy. Serve hot with a cooked grain and sautéed mushrooms. Use a half chicken breast for each serving.

For each serving:

1	half chicken breast, deboned, skinned and fat removed	1
2	broccoli florets	2
	Granulated onion	
	Granulated garlic	
	Season All	
2 tbsp	Barbecue Sauce (pg. 64)	25 mL
1 tsp	grated Parmesan cheese	5 mL
¼ cup	dry white wine	50 mL

Pound each chicken breast gently between waxed paper to thin slightly. Lay each breast on work surface, skin side down. Spice each with a sprinkle of onion, garlic and Season All.

Place 2 broccoli florets on chicken breast, with head of broccoli over the long edge and stems facing in. Roll breast, enclosing broccoli inside, leaving heads showing at each end; secure with toothpick. Place rolls in glass baking dish. On each roll, spread barbecue sauce; sprinkle with Parmesan. Pour wine into dish. Bake, covered, in 350°F (180°C) oven for 25 minutes.

Chicken Teriyaki

When the chicken breasts are skinned and boned and waiting in the freezer, this dish is very fast to prepare. Serve with lots of steamed fresh vegetables and steamed rice.

For each serving:

1	half chicken breast (or more if they are small)	1
1½ tbsp	sesame seed oil	20 mL
	Teriyaki Sauce (pg. 68) or commercial sauce	

Marinate chicken breasts in Teriyaki Sauce for at least 30 minutes or overnight in the refrigerator. In non-stick skillet with the sesame seed oil, sauté marinated chicken breasts on each side, about 3 to 4 minutes.

Roasted Chicken with Garlic and Herbs

This can be made with one or two whole cut-up chickens, or any combination of chicken parts. The breasts have the lowest calorie count.

1	cut-up roasting chicken or chicken parts (all skin and fat removed), cleaned and dried	1
3 tbsp	Dijon mustard	50 mL
1 tbsp	extra virgin olive oil	15 mL
1 tbsp	dried tarragon	15 mL
1 tbsp	prepared white horseradish	15 mL
1 tsp	freshly ground green peppercorns	5 mL
¼ cup	dry white wine	50 mL
1	large whole head garlic	1

Mix together mustard, oil, tarragon, horseradish and peppercorns. Brush mixture over chicken; place in roasting pan. Pour in wine.

Clean head of garlic. Arrange all cloves over chicken. Cover roaster with foil, shiny side up, and bake in 350°F (180°C) oven for 25 minutes. Remove cover and check moisture. A small amount of water may be added to pan if it appears to be drying out. Roast, uncovered, for 15 to 20 minutes longer. (Adjust timing for the quantity.)

Chicken Fire Steak

These are great on the barbecue, under the broiler or in a non-stick skillet. They can be made in quantity anytime, individually wrapped in waxed paper then bagged and frozen for later use. Serve with lots of steamed vegetables and brown rice for a fast, economical and low-calorie dinner. Allow about 4 oz (125 g) extra-lean ground chicken per steak.

	Skinless and boneless chicken breasts (Each breast will be large enough to handle 2 or 3 chicken steaks; calculate the number of breasts based on amount of minced chicken being prepared.)	
1 lb	extra-lean ground chicken	500 g
1	egg (or 2 egg whites) (to a maximum of 5 whites)	1
2 tbsp	Worcestershire sauce	25 mL
3 tbsp	prepared mustard	50 mL
1 tbsp	granulated garlic	15 mL
1 tbsp	granulated onion	15 mL
1 tbsp	Season All	15 mL
½ cup	bread crumbs	125 mL
¼ cup	(approx) water	50 mL
3 or 4	green or white peppercorns	3 or 4
	Granulated garlic	

In large bowl, mix ground chicken, egg, Worcestershire sauce, mustard, garlic, onion, Season All, bread crumbs and water. Adjust amount of water so meat holds together. Set aside.

Wash each chicken breast in cool water; drain on paper towel. Place one chicken breast between two sheets of waxed paper; gently flatten breast (not too thin), using bottom of drinking glass or mallet, to even out thickness and elongate shape. Depending on size of breast, cut each into 2 or 3 long strips approximately 1 inch (2.5 cm) wide.

Divide ground chicken mixture into 4-oz (125 g) balls; flatten slightly with heel of your hand. Wrap each chicken ball with 1 chicken strip; secure with toothpick. Slightly flatten chicken steak a bit more with the heel of your hand to make a bond with chicken strip.

In piece of waxed paper, using rolling pin, crush peppercorns (adjust quantity according to the amount of steaks being made). To crushed peppercorns, add 1 tsp (5 mL) granulated garlic for each tbsp (15 mL) of peppercorns. Mix well.

Roll edge of each chicken steak in peppercorn-garlic mix. The Chicken Fire Steak may be cooked immediately or frozen.

Chicken Strip Sauté

This creative dinner is adapted from a traditional stir-fry. The large amount of oil used in the wok has been eliminated. If you do not have a wok, a large skillet will work equally well. The quantities given here will serve 4 people; amounts may be adjusted for more or fewer. Serve with steamed rice.

2	whole chicken breasts, cut in long thin strips	2
1 tsp	granulated garlic	5 mL
1 tsp	granulated onion	5 mL
1 tbsp	sesame seed oil	15 mL
1/3 cup	water	75 mL
1 tbsp	low-sodium chicken soup powder	15 mL
3 tbsp	low-sodium soy sauce	50 mL
2 tbsp	granulated onion	25 mL
1/4 tsp	white pepper	1 mL
1/4 tsp	ground ginger	1 mL
1	onion, sliced	1
4 to 8 cups	fresh bean sprouts	1 to 2 L

1 cup	thickly sliced mushrooms	250 mL
1 cup	broccoli florets or snow peas	250 mL

Sprinkle chicken strips with garlic and onion; set aside.

Heat sesame seed oil in wok or large skillet. In small measuring cup, mix together water, chicken soup powder, soy sauce, onion, white pepper and ginger. Set aside.

In wok, sauté chicken strips and sliced onion until chicken is almost cooked, about 3 to 4 minutes. Add ¼ cup (50 mL) chicken soup liquid, mushrooms and broccoli. Cover; cook for 2 minutes.

Remove chicken and vegetables to a plate or bowl; set aside. (The following may be divided in 2 batches if the pan is too small to hold it all.) Place bean sprouts in wok. Pour in remaining chicken soup liquid; toss with bean sprouts. Cook until tender-crisp. In large bowl, toss sprouts with chicken-vegetable mixture. Makes 4 servings.

Note:
It is best to undercook the bean sprouts, as they can easily be reheated in a microwave oven before serving without damaging the texture.

Bountiful Beautiful Vegetables

Cooking and Buying Vegetables

Steaming retains vitamins, adds no calories and leaves vegetables with a bright appetizing color. Steaming meat reduces shrinkage, and fat drips into the steaming liquid; this can be skimmed off. Water, wine or broth can be used for the steaming liquid, and any number and types of herbs or spices can be added. The steaming liquid can then be reduced and used as sauce, or thickened to a gravy. Meat, poultry and fish can all be steamed without fat, and they retain a moist tenderness. Even tough inexpensive cuts can become tender and moist.

There are many fancy steamers on the market, but the simplest steamer is an inexpensive stainless steel or plastic (not aluminum) adjustable steamer basket. For the serious-minded, there are three- and four-story steaming pots that allow you to steam an entire dinner at the same time. Foods are arranged in order of steaming times, with the meats on the lowest level, root vegetables next and leafy greens and fruits on the top. Whichever method you choose, the health benefits of steaming vegetables, along with the increased flavor, will sell you on this method.

Microwave cooking, like steaming, retains the vitamins and color of the vegetables. If a microwave oven is being used, follow the manufacturer's directions given with your oven, remembering that times can vary depending on the amount being cooked, the temperature of the food and the wattage or power of your microwave oven.

With microwave cooking, remember to allow for standing time; food will continue to cook after it is removed from the oven. To stop the cooking, rinse just-cooked vegetables under cold water.

Salt should never be used when microwaving vegetables. The flavor is really quite fantastic when steaming or microwave steaming is used. Small amounts of herbs or spices may be added after cooking, and a little grated Parmesan cheese adds a special flavor without the calories and fat of cheese sauces.

Boiling, with a few exceptions, should be avoided. Vegetables will not retain their vitamin content and, without careful monitoring, can become overcooked. The flavors are lost when vegetables are boiled.

The key word here is FRESH! Avoid canned vegetables. They are loaded with salt. In a pinch, when fresh ones are hard to get, buy frozen (and remember to adjust cooking times). And if the vegetable you want is not available or is of poor quality, use a similar-type vegetable instead. Some types of fresh vegetables are usually available at all times of the year.

There are a few exceptions to the rule against canned vegetables. Canned stewed tomatoes (low-sodium) are preferable to poor-quality fresh and certainly more economical (and flavorful) in the winter. Keeping on hand a stock of canned cooked lentils and beans of all types will allow you to add these items to many recipes — without taking the time to soak the beans or extend cooking times. (Rinse them well; a five-minute soak in cold water will remove a great deal of the sodium.)

Asparagus

Avoid plastic-wrapped bunches. Look for thin (no thicker than your baby finger), straight stalks with compact pointed tips. The freshest asparagus is crisp to the touch. The bottom should have only a scant inch (2.5 cm) of white fiber with pink overtones. Store with the stalk ends wrapped in wet paper towels in a plastic bag for no more than 2 to 3 days in the refrigerator.

Asparagus should be peeled (unless it is pencil thin) to remove the tough outer skin that is hard to digest. Before peeling, break off (do not cut) the bottom part of the stalk at the point where it snaps off easily. Do not peel to the top; stop about halfway up the stalk. Wash the asparagus in a large basin of cold water, as sand can sometimes get into the tips.

Asparagus can be steamed in small bunches standing upright in a covered deep pot with water to the depth of 1 inch (2.5 cm); herbs can be added to the water. Over medium heat, cooking will take approximately 10 minutes, even less if the asparagus is very thin and very fresh. Asparagus can also be cooked in a large saucepan on top of the stove, half filled with water, for 3 to 5 minutes. Be careful not to overcook; they should be barely tender.

Microwave steaming works well. Place the asparagus flat in a microwave-safe container that will hold it comfortably (do not overcrowd); alternate tips and ends. I use a microwave-safe glass loaf pan. Pour into the container 2 tbsp (25 mL) water or dry white wine; cover with a lid or plastic wrap. The timing will vary depending on the amount being cooked and the thickness of the stalks. Follow your manufacturer's rules for microwaved vegetables.

If the asparagus is being served cold, it should be cooled down immediately after cooking, under cold running water. Drain and pat dry with paper towels before serving.

Cold Asparagus with Yogurt-Mustard Sauce

	Asparagus	
½ cup	skim-milk yogurt	125 mL
2 tbsp	Dijon mustard	25 mL
1 tbsp	lemon juice	15 mL
½ tsp	granulated onion	2 mL

Prepare asparagus and cool in water. (Some ice cubes in the water will speed the process.) Pat dry with paper towel; place asparagus on a long dish or platter.

Blend yogurt, mustard, lemon juice and onion. Pour over asparagus.

Plain Steamed Asparagus

Try some of the following to enhance the fresh flavor of cooked asparagus.

Squeeze some fresh lemon juice over cooked stalks, and sprinkle with 3 tbsp (50 mL) grated Parmesan cheese.

After squeezing fresh lemon juice on the asparagus, sprinkle with ½ tsp (2 mL) granulated garlic (grated Parmesan can also be used).

Mix together 1½ tsp (7 mL) low-sodium soy sauce, ½ tsp (2 mL) sesame seed oil and ¼ tsp (1 mL) ground ginger. Sprinkle over the asparagus.

Bean Sprouts

Look for sprouts that are whitish, with no traces of brown. The sprouts should be crisp, not limp. Refrigerate sprouts in a plastic bag to prevent them from drying out. If storage will be for more than a day or two, blanch the sprouts. This will stop the maturing process and keep them firm for several more days.

Rinse sprouts under cold water; drain. To blanch sprouts: place them in a colander in the sink; pour about 8 cups (2 L) of boiling water over sprouts. Follow with a rinse of cold water to stop the cooking. Drain well. Store in a plastic bag in the refrigerator.

Chinese-Style Bean Sprouts

1 tbsp	sesame seed oil	15 mL
1	onion, cut in half, then sliced thickly	1
4 to 5 cups	washed and drained fresh bean sprouts	1 to 1.25 L
1 tbsp	granulated onion	15 mL
1 tsp	ground ginger	5 mL
½ tsp	white pepper	2 mL
¼ cup	low-sodium soy sauce	50 mL

Heat wok or skillet. Pour sesame oil into pan; move pan around to coat it.

Cook onion in wok until onion starts to wilt, 2 to 3 minutes. Add bean sprouts; sprinkle with granulated onion, ginger and pepper. Stir bean sprouts to distribute spice. Pour in soy sauce; continue to stir sprouts as they cook. Cook sprouts for 3 to 4 minutes; be careful not to overcook. Serves 4 to 5 as a side dish.

Variations:
The following may be added to this basic recipe:

• 1 cup (250 mL) chopped leftover cooked chicken
• Small amounts of shrimp; scallops; or chopped well-drained tofu that has been cooked in 1 tsp (5 mL) sesame oil and 2 tbsp (25 mL) soy sauce before adding onions and sprouts.

Broccoli
Always look for fresh unpackaged broccoli. Fresh broccoli has tightly closed blue-green florets or buds, with dark green firm stalks. Avoid yellowing or wilted buds and open-cored branches. Avoid rubbery and wilted broccoli; it should feel crisp. Avoid strong-smelling broccoli; it will smell even stronger when it is cooked.

Take care never to overcook broccoli. The stalks can be peeled, even sliced, and cooked. I also use the lower stalks if the broccoli is very fresh and not overly thick (these will be very tender and taste great). The tops should be carefully washed and steamed. Steaming on the stove should not take more than 4 to 5 minutes; the microwave oven will take less time. Adjustments in timing will need to be made for quantity and freshness.

Plain Steamed Broccoli

Cooked broccoli can be enhanced with any combination of fresh-squeezed lemon juice, grated Parmesan cheese, granulated garlic and granulated onion.

After cooking broccoli, toss it with 1½ tsp (7 mL) extra virgin olive oil mixed with ½ tsp (2 mL) granulated garlic, 1 tbsp (15 mL) white wine and ½ tsp (2 mL) chili powder.

Over plain steamed broccoli, sprinkle 2 tbsp (25 mL) grated Parmesan cheese.

Tip:
To sweeten some not-so-fresh broccoli, place 2 tbsp (25 mL) white wine in the bottom of the cooking dish before microwaving.

Broccoli with Garlic

Slice cloves of 1 whole head of garlic; sauté in 1 tsp (5 mL) virgin olive oil until softened. Toss garlic into steamed broccoli with 2 tbsp (25 mL) grated Parmesan cheese. Serve warm or cold.

Brussels Sprouts
Look for small, firm, dark green sprouts with tight leaves. Avoid yellowing or rusted leaves–a sign of an old sprout, and the taste will be strong and unpleasant. Store loosely wrapped in the refrigerator for up to 1 week.

Pull off any loose leaves and trim the stem. A tiny X cut in the base of each sprout with a sharp knife will allow faster cooking.

Brussels sprouts can be steamed on top of the stove, 12 to 15 minutes; the microwave oven will take 4 to 5 minutes. These times will vary with size and quantity. After cooking, plunge sprouts into cold water to stop the cooking. The only thing that tastes worse than an old sprout is one that has been overcooked.

If the sprouts are less than very fresh, or if they were stored in the refrigerator a few extra days before using, try this method to revive and sweeten them. After washing and preparing, place the sprouts in a container filled with water and ¼ to ½ cup (50 mL to 125 mL) instant skim-milk powder. Soak for at least 30 minutes and drain before cooking.

Sliced Brussels Sprouts with Parmesan

	Brussels sprouts	
1 tbsp	virgin olive oil	15 mL
	Lemon juice	
1 tsp	granulated garlic	5 mL
4 to 5 tbsp	grated Parmesan cheese	50 to 75 mL
½ cup	chopped sweet red pepper (optional)	125 mL

Steam brussels sprouts until they are almost cooked. Plunge them into cold water to stop cooking; drain.

Slice sprouts lengthwise into ¼-inch (5 mm) slices. Sauté sprouts in olive oil; sprinkle with lemon juice and garlic. Add Parmesan cheese; sauté for 2 to 3 minutes in total. Transfer to serving dish. (Optional: sauté sweet red pepper in olive oil for 2 minutes before adding brussels sprouts.)

Dilled Brussels Sprouts

	Brussels sprouts	
1 tbsp	extra virgin olive oil	15 mL
1 tbsp	dry white wine	15 mL
Pinch	freshly ground pepper	Pinch
1 tsp	dried dill	5 mL

Steam brussels sprouts; drain and set aside. Mix together remaining ingredients. Toss with sprouts. Serve warm.

Cabbage

Look for firm, smooth and tightly packed leaves indicating a young and tasty cabbage. A split in a cabbage is a sign of age, and so is a strong cabbage odor. Cabbage stores well in a plastic bag for 1 to 2 weeks in the refrigerator.

Cabbage can be steamed, braised, baked or stir-fried. If you find the cooking odor of cabbage too strong, toss a stalk of celery or an English walnut into the pot. Cabbage can be used in other recipes in many roles. Here we will deal with cabbage as an accompaniment to a meal.

1 firm medium-sized head = about 2 lb (1 kg) or about 8 cups (2 L) shredded

Steamed or Blanched Cabbage

Remove and discard the tough outer leaves; cut the head into quarters. Core it by cutting out the hard center at the base. Slice the quarters into ¼-inch (5 mm) slices.

To blanch: place cabbage in a pot (not aluminum) with enough water to cover. Boil, uncovered, for 5 to 8 minutes. Do not overcook; it should be al dente. Rinse cooked cabbage under cold water to stop the cooking.

Two cups (500 mL) of shredded cabbage takes about 4½ minutes to cook, covered, at High power in a microwave oven.

Baked Cabbage and Apples

1 tbsp	virgin olive oil	15 mL
1	leek (white and light green part only), sliced	1
6 cups	shredded cabbage	1.5 L
2	unpeeled apples, grated	2
1	onion, finely diced	1
¼ tsp	freshly ground pepper	1 mL
½ cup	shredded extra-old low-fat Cheddar cheese	125 mL
¼ cup	dry bread crumbs	50 mL

Heat oil in large skillet; sauté leek over medium heat. Add cabbage; cook, stirring constantly, for 5 to 6 minutes, until barely tender. Add apples, onion and pepper; cook for about 2 minutes. Pour mixture into shallow casserole or baking dish. Top cabbage with Cheddar and bread crumbs. Bake, uncovered, in 375°F (190°C) oven until top is browned. Makes 4 to 5 servings.

Cauliflower
Look for a white head with tightly packed flowers and fresh green leaves. Avoid strong-smelling heads and excessively crumbly cauliflower. If the head is fresh, it will have only a faint cabbage scent. If the flesh has discolored, or the leaves have grayed, the vegetable can be tough and chewy; loose or spreading florets mean the cauliflower is over-mature.

For the freshest cauliflowers: remove the tough outer leaves; hollow out the core using a sharp knife. The head can be blanched in a pot of boiling water. Place the head down and keep the pot uncovered. Cooking time will depend on the weight and size, but 8 to 12 minutes will usually be enough for blanching.

Less than the freshest (ones that have been in cold storage) cauliflowers usually develop a stronger flavor. A soaking in cold water with 1 tsp (5 mL) vinegar for at least half an hour before cooking will remove excessive acidity. Two tbsp (25 mL) dry white wine added to the container of cauliflower before microwaving will sweeten a less-than-fresh head. The best method I have found, if time permits, is to soak cauliflower in water to cover (mixed with ½ cup/125 mL skim-milk powder per 2 to 3 cups/500 mL to 750 mL water) for at least 30 minutes. (Soak overnight for use the following day.) This will revive and sweeten the flavor of an older cauliflower.

To microwave: place the whole head of cauliflower in a microwave-safe container. Pour 2 tbsp (25 mL) dry white wine into container; cover with a lid or plastic wrap. Microwave for 5 to 10 minutes (depending on the size). Remove before cauliflower is fully cooked; it will continue to cook as it stands. To stop the cooking, rinse well with cold water.

Steamed Cauliflower with Parmesan

Steam or microwave cauliflower after it has soaked in skim milk for at least 30 minutes, or cook with 2 tbsp (25 mL) white wine in microwave oven. Before serving, sprinkle with 2 tbsp (25 mL) grated Parmesan. (The cauliflower can be steamed with some of the soaking liquid — milk, or water and vinegar — as the steaming liquid.)

Carrots
For the freshest carrots, look for the ones with the green tops. Old carrots are usually cracked and brittle and send out tiny white roots. Avoid limp carrots, and those with very thick tops tapering to thin roots (these tend to be bitter).

Baby carrots have been showing up in the supermarket. For the privilege of paying more, you are losing out on carotene, the dark coloring, which is converted to vitamin A in our body. They are, however, decorative on a dinner plate.

Carrots will store in the refrigerator in a plastic bag for up to a month.

Peeling is usually done with all but baby carrots, though many prefer to scrub well and not peel. Let freshness be your guide. There are many methods of preparation, depending on the recipe — sliced, diced, julienne, shredded, chunks, or left whole.

Grated carrots can be frozen without any preparation (blanching or steaming) and can be thawed and used in salads, or added to cooked or baked dishes, breads, cookies and cakes.

Note:
Keep a plastic bag of peeled and washed carrot sticks handy in the refrigerator, along with celery sticks. They make great munchies for kids just before dinner when they are too hungry to wait. Carrots are good munchies anytime, and will help the dieting cook get through dinner preparation without snacking on the food. (Keep the carrots to a minimum if you are on a diet.)

> 1 lb (500 g) carrots, shredded = 4 cups (1 L)
> 2 carrots, shredded = 1 cup (250 mL)
> 2 carrots, cut into coins = 1 cup (250 mL)

Steamed Carrots with a Variety of Flavors

Carrots have a high sugar content. That natural sweetness can be used along with subtle flavors to create simple yet interesting new tastes for the old carrot.

Slice 4 to 6 carrots into ¼-inch (5 mm) rounds. Steam in the microwave oven with 2 tbsp (25 mL) water for 5 to 7 minutes. Or steam in a steaming basket or colander over a pot of boiling water for 8 to 10 minutes. Carrots should remain barely tender to the fork, not soft or mushy.

Toss cooked carrots with one of the following: 2 tbsp (25 mL) lemon juice; 2 tbsp (25 mL) orange juice; 2 tbsp (25 mL) lime juice; ½ tsp (2 mL) dried tarragon; 2 tbsp (25 mL) chopped fresh parsley; 1 tbsp (15 mL) apricot brandy.

Glazed Carrots

1 lb	carrots (about 4 to 6), sliced in ¼-inch (5 mm) rounds	500 g
¾ cup	cold water	175 mL
1 tbsp	cornstarch	15 mL
¼ cup	orange juice	50 mL
1 tbsp	brandy or brandy flavoring	15 mL

Steam carrots until barely fork tender.

In a saucepan, stir together water, cornstarch, orange juice and brandy; cook until thickened. Add carrots. Heat until well coated. Serve hot. Makes 4 to 5 servings.

Carrots and Minted Peas

4	carrots, grated	4
1 cup	fresh or frozen peas	250 mL
1 tbsp	crème de menthe or mint flavoring	15 mL

Steam carrots and peas together for 2 to 3 minutes; be careful not to overcook. Drain any excess liquid. Stir in crème de menthe. Serve hot. Makes 4 servings.

Notes:

• Fresh or dried mint can be substituted for crème de menthe.
• Leftover cooked carrots can be puréed and frozen in an ice-cube tray, then bagged. Toss several into soup, gravy, chili and baking.

Corn

Look for very grassy green husks; the silk should be no darker than deep amber. Peel back the husk; the kernels should look moist, be set in even rows and be plump but not too large. Check the stem end; if it has rusted, the corn is old and will not taste good.

For boiling: Clean away the husk and silk; wash cob with cold water. Place in a pot. Cover with water and add a pinch of sugar. If the corn is not fresh from the farm, boil it in a mixture of ½ cup (125 mL) skim-milk powder per 2 to 3 cups (500 mL to 750 mL) water.

Skim-milk soaking makes corn taste as though it had just been picked. If the corn is being steamed in the microwave oven, or barbecued, soak cobs in a mixture of ½ cup (125 mL) skim-milk powder per 2 to 3 cups (500 mL to 750 mL) water for at least 1 hour before cooking.

For baking: pull down the husk carefully but do not fully remove it. Remove the silk and wash the corn. Rub corn with a very sparing amount of margarine; rewrap the corn in the husks. (Aluminum foil can substitute for the husks.) Bake for about 20 minutes in a 350°F (180°C) oven. The corn can also be barbecued this way.

To microwave: Prepare the corn in the husks as for baking. (Never use aluminum foil in the microwave oven.) The corn can also be cooked without the husks in a covered container. Usually 3 to 4 minutes per cob is required.

To remove kernels from the cob: Stand an ear of corn upright on a cutting surface; carefully slice beneath the kernels with a downward motion.

To grate kernels from the cob: Cut off the tops of the kernels, and with the back of the blade scrape off what is left on the cob.

Sautéed Corn and Mushrooms

1½ tsp	virgin olive oil	7 mL
1	onion, finely chopped	1
2	cloves garlic, minced	2
3 cups	fresh or frozen corn kernels	750 mL
1 cup	sliced mushrooms	250 mL
1 tsp	dried thyme	5 mL
½ tsp	freshly ground white pepper	2 mL

Sauté onion and garlic in olive oil for 3 minutes. Stir in corn, mushrooms, thyme and pepper. Cook, covered, for 5 minutes. Makes 5 to 6 servings.

Baked Whiskey Creamed Corn

3 cups	fresh or frozen corn	750 mL
1	small onion, finely chopped	1
1	potato, peeled and cut in ½-inch (1 cm) cubes	1
3 tbsp	whiskey	50 mL
1 cup	skim milk	250 mL
2 tbsp	cornstarch	25 mL
¼ cup	instant skim-milk powder	50 mL
¼ tsp	white pepper	1 mL
4 tsp	low-sodium chicken soup powder	20 mL

In 4-cup (1 L) oven-proof casserole, place corn, onion, potato and whiskey. Mix well. In 2-cup (500 mL) measure, mix together milk, cornstarch, milk powder, pepper and chicken soup powder; pour over corn, mixing well. Bake, covered, for 15 minutes. Remove casserole from oven; stir corn mixture well. Cover; return to oven. Bake in 350°F (180°C) oven for 15 to 20 minutes. Serve hot. (This dish reheats well the next day.) Makes 4 to 5 servings.

Green Beans

Look for unblemished, crisp, firm beans that are bright fresh-looking green. Avoid limp, soggy-looking beans that appear to be swollen with seeds. Pencil-thin beans are the sweetest and indicate a young bean.

Young pencil-thin beans can be left whole. Large mature beans can be cut into french-style strips, chopped or cut on an angle. Beans can be steamed, blanched or microwaved with excellent results.

> 1 lb (500 g) untrimmed whole beans = 4 cups (1 L) trimmed cut beans = 3½ cups (875 mL) trimmed and finely diced

Sautéed Green Beans with Mushrooms

1 tbsp	virgin olive oil	15 mL
½ to ¾ lb	fresh green beans (pencil-thin if available)	250 to 375 g
Half	sweet red pepper, chopped	Half
1 cup	thickly sliced mushrooms	250 mL
½ tsp	freshly ground green peppercorns	2 mL
½ tsp	granulated garlic	2 mL
1	chicken ice-cube (or 4 tsp/20 mL) water mixed with ½ tsp/2 mL low-sodium chicken soup powder)	1

In non-stick skillet over medium heat, heat olive oil. Sauté green beans and red pepper for 3 to 4 minutes. Add mushrooms, green peppercorns, garlic and chicken ice-cube. Cover; steam for 5 minutes. Serve hot. Makes 4 to 5 servings.

Variation:
The mushrooms may be replaced with grated carrots.

Green Beans with Garlic

2 tbsp	low-sodium soy sauce	25 mL
1 tbsp	dry white wine (optional)	15 mL
1½ tsp	sesame seed oil	7 mL
1 lb	green beans, cut diagonally in 2-inch (5 cm) lengths	500 g
Half	head garlic, cloves sliced	Half
1 tsp	ground ginger	5 mL
1 tbsp	toasted sesame seeds (optional)	15 mL

In bowl, mix together soy sauce and wine (if using); set aside.
In wok or skillet over medium heat, heat sesame oil. Add
beans and garlic. Sprinkle with ginger. Cook, stirring, for 2
minutes. Stir in soy mixture; cook, covered, until beans are
tender-crisp, about 7 minutes.

Uncover; increase heat. Continue to cook and stir until
liquid has almost evaporated. Serve warm with toasted sesame
seeds sprinkled on top, if desired. Makes 4 to 5 servings.

Mushrooms

Look for loose mushrooms, not the prepackaged ones. Select
mushrooms that are firm with short stems, unblemished and
without gray spots. Avoid mushrooms that are open
underneath exposing the gills; these are not fresh. Size is only
important to the use of the mushrooms.

There have always been many opinions about the best
method for cleaning mushrooms. Some experts tell us to only
wipe the dirt away or use a mushroom brush for that
purpose. Some say to peel the mushrooms. Still others say do
not peel but wash the mushrooms. One point is true: if water
is used, it should be kept to a minimum. Whichever method
you use, never clean the mushrooms when they are
purchased. Store unwashed, loosely wrapped in the
refrigerator, for up to 5 days. Clean them just before use.

Mushrooms with Herbs

2 tsp	virgin olive oil	10 mL
½ tsp	dried tarragon, basil, oregano or marjoram	2 mL
1 lb	whole mushrooms (small to medium)	500 g

In skillet, combine oil, herbs and mushrooms; cook until mushrooms are tender and have just started to let out juices. Be careful not to overcook the mushrooms.

(To microwave: Place oil in 8-cup/2 L casserole; stir in herbs. Stir in mushrooms. Microwave, uncovered, at High for 4 to 6 minutes until tender and juices have just started to be released.)

Quick Mushroom Sauce

1 tsp	virgin olive oil	5 mL
½ lb	mushrooms, sliced	250 g
1 tbsp	flour	15 mL
1 cup	cold broth (beef or chicken)	250 mL
	Frozen broth cubes	
	Freshly ground pepper	
1 tbsp	dry white wine (optional)	15 mL

In small pot, stir olive oil and mushrooms. Cook on high heat only long enough for mushrooms to let out their juices. Remove from heat.

Blend flour into cold broth. In cold broth, melt some frozen broth cubes (or mix in some low-sodium broth powder). Stir mixture into mushrooms; cook over medium heat. Add pepper and wine (if using). Cook only until sauce thickens. Makes 2 cups (500 mL).

Quick Sautéed Mushrooms

1 tbsp	virgin olive oil	15 mL
1 lb	button mushrooms or large mushrooms sliced thickly	500 g
1 tsp	granulated garlic	5 mL
	Freshly ground green or white pepper	
3 tbsp	grated Parmesan cheese	50 mL

Heat olive oil in skillet. Add mushrooms, garlic and pepper; stir. Cook just until mushrooms start to release liquid. Remove to serving dish; sprinkle with Parmesan. Serve at once. Makes 4 servings.

Leftovers can be processed, thickened with flour and turned into gravy with the addition of a small amount of soup stock.

Onions

Look for odorless onions with papery dry skins. Avoid onions that have begun to sprout. The one onion available year-round is the yellow or golden globe. The size will vary, but this has nothing to do with its flavor. This onion works well in all recipes.

White or pearl onions are small and sweet. These are most often used whole in stews or casseroles. The baby pearls are usually used in a cocktail. Spanish onions are very mild, but require cooking to eliminate a bitter undertaste.

Bermuda onions are very sweet and can be eaten raw; they are great on hamburgers. Red onions are the mildest; this sweet onion is the best to use raw in salads.

Leeks are best when they are not larger than 2 inches (5 cm) in diameter. Larger leeks are tough and the flavor becomes rather strong with lengthy cooking. However, large leeks can be used in soups. Trim the leek, allowing only 2 inches (5 cm) of green to remain.

Over the years, I have tried many methods to prevent the onion's acid spray from bringing tears to my eyes. None of them have been fully successful except for using my daughter's scuba diving mask. This is neither comfortable nor practical. Wearing some type of protection over the eyes does seem to be the answer. A pair of plastic eye protectors that can be found in a hardware store will do the job — and are more comfortable than a scuba mask.

Tiny white onions should be placed in a pot of boiling water for 30 seconds, then plunged into cold water. This will loosen the skin; a shallow X cut at the root end of the onion will ensure even cooking. Leeks should be bathed in lukewarm water. Fill the sink with the water and let the leeks soak until a good deal of grit has come out. Fan out the leaves and hold the leeks under cold running water to finish cleaning.

Note:

To tame any onion for use raw, cover onion slices with a half-and-half mixture of water and vinegar and soak overnight, refrigerated. Herbs may also be mixed into the liquid.

> 1 onion = 1½ cups (375 mL) chopped
>   = 2 cups (500 mL) thinly sliced
> 3 large onions = 2 lb (1 kg)
> 3 medium onions = 1 lb (500 g)
> 7 small onions = 1 lb (500 g)

Braised Onions with Scotch

Serve these onions hot with beef, veal or chicken. Great on top of a burger.

3	onions (cooking or Spanish)	3
3 tbsp	Scotch	50 mL

Cut onions in half; cut in ¼-inch (5 mm) slices.

Lightly coat non-stick pan with olive oil spray. When pan is hot, add onions; sauté until golden. Stir in Scotch; continue cooking for 2 to 3 minutes. Makes 4 to 5 servings.

Variation:
Add sliced mushrooms just before the Scotch is added.

Baked Barbecued Onions

3 to 4	onions	3 to 4
1 cup	Barbecue Sauce (pg. 64)	250 mL
¼ cup	dry white wine	50 mL

Slice onions into ½-inch (1 cm) slices. Layer onions in large shallow baking dish. Blend Barbecue Sauce with wine. Spread thin layer of sauce over each layer. Bake, covered, in 350°F (180°C) oven for 15 minutes; remove cover and bake for 30 minutes to brown. Makes 4 to 5 servings.

Green Peas
Look for pods that will snap, not bend, under slight pressure. Always select ones with the brightest color. Old pods are usually frayed around the edges, and over-mature ones bulge and form ridges on the pod. Store loosely wrapped for up to 2 days.

Fresh peas hold their vitamins better if they are not overcooked. Bring a pot of water to a boil and drop the shelled peas into the pot; cook for 1 minute. Do not wait for the water to return to the boil; drain peas and rinse under cold water. The peas are ready to use in any recipe, or save them to reheat for use later.

Commercially frozen peas are what I use, since fresh are not always available and I usually don't have time to shell fresh ones. NEVER boil frozen peas; these only need to be heated to be eaten. Frozen peas are very close to fresh in taste, so be careful not to overcook them.

For use as an addition in another recipe, frozen peas may be added almost at the end of cooking time.

Peas with Mushrooms and Herbs

Frozen peas go well with mushrooms — both require little cooking time and make a great taste combination.

4	cloves garlic, sliced	4
1 tbsp	virgin olive oil	15 mL
½ lb	mushrooms (small to medium)	250 g
1½ cups	frozen green peas	375 g
1 tsp	dried tarragon	5 mL
1 tbsp	dry white wine (optional)	15 mL

Sauté garlic in olive oil until cloves start to brown. Add mushrooms; cook for about 30 seconds. Stir in green peas, tarragon and wine (if using). Sauté for about 2 minutes. Makes 4 servings.

Peppers

Look for firm, bright peppers. They should have weight to them, which indicates a good water content. Sweet peppers are usually referred to as "bells," because of their shape. Red bell peppers are no hotter than the green ones. The redness only indicates ripeness; these peppers are a bit sweeter than the green ones. All bell peppers are mild. No matter which color is used, they will all give the dish the right degree of flavor.

Chili peppers come in a multitude of shapes and sizes with varying degrees of heat. What makes a chili pepper hot is within its seeds and pale interior spines. When both are removed, the chili is a mild vegetable. Some varieties are so fiery that you should wear rubber gloves when preparing them to avoid burns on your hands. These peppers should be used sparingly in any recipe.

Peppers are a versatile food, and there are no hard and fast rules for preparing them. Peppers can be eaten raw, roasted, sautéed, blanched — it depends on how they are to be used in the recipe.

Roasted Peppers

Peppers can be roasted under the broiler, in a hot oven or over the barbecue grill. Whichever method is used, the peppers are prepared in the same way.

Cut peppers in half, and core and seed them.

Broiling: Place peppers on broiler pan about 5 inches (12 cm) below broiler; turn often until peppers are charred on both sides (about 25 minutes). When peppers are done, pop them into paper bag and close bag tightly. This will allow skins to steam off in about 20 minutes. Using sharp paring knife, remove skins. Hold peppers under cold water to further loosen skins if they give you any trouble.

Baking: Place peppers on a baking sheet in a 400°F (200°C) oven; roast for 15 minutes on each side. Continue with procedure to remove skins.

Grilling: Place peppers on barbecue grill; turn when they are blistered and well charred. Continue with procedure to remove skins.

Using Roasted Peppers

Place roasted pepper halves on a baking sheet; sprinkle with 1 tbsp (15 mL) shredded skim-milk mozzarella cheese and 1 tsp (5 mL) grated Parmesan cheese; sprinkle with fresh or dried chives. Broil until cheese melts. Serve with crusty bread and a bowl of hearty soup like Beef and Barley (pg. 49).

Cut peppers into strips to use in salads, or to toss with fish and pasta.

Make a purée from peppers; add just enough extra virgin olive oil for flavor; add herbs and garlic. Use as a pesto on pasta, or float a tablespoon (15 mL) of pepper pesto on the surface of soup as a garnish and for flavor. The pepper purée may be frozen in an ice-cube tray; bag pepper cubes and thaw for instant red pepper anytime.

Note:
When red peppers are plentiful and inexpensive, they may be chopped, bagged and frozen in recipe-size quantities. This is also a good time to make and freeze red pepper pesto.

Potatoes
Look for firm, clean potatoes that have weight and are smooth to the touch. Avoid any that are sprouting, bruised, soft or patched with green. A green-patched potato is not underripe; it is bitter. If you spot a green patch on a potato, cut the area away.

There are more than 400 varieties of potatoes. Old (high-starch) potatoes are prime for the skillet, baking or frying. New (low-starch) potatoes have a firm texture and thin skin. They are best for boiling, roasting, casseroles and salads.

What type of potato you choose will determine the results. Use the low-starch for boiling, especially if you are going to mash them. Use the high-starch for baking or frying. Baked potatoes can be done with or without a foil wrapping. The skin will be crunchier if foil is not used. To obtain the ultimate crunchy skin, place the potato under the broiler (without foil) after it has baked; let the skin become brown-burned. The same can be done on the barbecue.

Mustard-Coated Potatoes

3 cups	(approx) tiny new potatoes, scrubbed	750 mL
2 tbsp	Dijon mustard	25 mL
2 tbsp	prepared mustard	25 mL
1 tsp	dry mustard	5 mL
1 tbsp	green peppercorns, crushed	15 mL
2 tbsp	minced fresh parsley (or 2 tsp/10 mL dried)	25 mL
1 tbsp	virgin olive oil	15 mL
2 tbsp	tequila (optional)	25 mL

Peel off a thin strip of skin around center of each potato.
Steam potatoes, or microwave until just tender. Drain off any
liquid. Mix together remaining ingredients; stir sauce into
potatoes. Keep potatoes warm in ovenproof dish in warm
oven, or reheat in microwave. This dish improves with age;
let flavors blend by preparing hours before using or even the
day before. Makes 4 servings.

Cottage-Cheese Stuffed Potatoes

4	baked potatoes	4
½ cup	skim milk	125 mL
1 tbsp	granulated onion	15 mL
¼ tsp	white pepper	1 mL
2 tbsp	minced fresh parsley (or 2 tsp/10 mL dried)	25 mL
1 cup	low-fat (1%) cottage cheese	250 mL
3 to 4 tbsp	grated Parmesan cheese	50 mL

Split baked potatoes open lengthwise; carefully scoop out
pulp into bowl. Mash potatoes with milk, onion, pepper and
parsley. Mix in cottage cheese. Fill each potato shell heaping
with mixture. Sprinkle with Parmesan cheese. Bake in 350°F
(180°C) oven until tops are golden.

Fantastic Oven-Roasted Potatoes

3 cups	peeled potatoes, cut in 2-inch (5 cm) chunks	750 mL
2 tsp	granulated onion	10 mL
2 tsp	granulated garlic	10 mL
1	onion, coarsely chopped	1
2 tbsp	virgin olive oil	25 mL
1 tbsp	beef concentrate	15 mL
2 tbsp	Scotch (optional)	25 mL

In oven-proof dish, combine potatoes, granulated onion and garlic. Mix in chopped onion. Pour in olive oil, beef concentrate and Scotch (if using), stirring well to coat. Bake in 350°F (180°C) oven until potatoes are tender and well browned, about 40 minutes; stir potatoes several times during roasting. Makes 4 servings.

Potato Cakes

Make these in quantity. They can be used as a side dish for dinner, or for breakfast served with applesauce or skim-milk yogurt. Make them bite-sized and serve as an hors d'oeuvre with a half-and-half mixture of Dijon mustard and skim-milk yogurt.

2 cups	cooked mashed potatoes	500 mL
1 cup	fast-cooking rolled oats	250 mL
1	egg (or 2 egg whites)	1
2 tsp	granulated onion	10 mL
4 tsp	Season All	20 mL
1/4 tsp	white pepper	1 mL
1/4 cup	skim-milk yogurt	50 mL
1 1/2 tsp	virgin olive oil or pan spray	7 mL

In large bowl, mix together all ingredients except oil. In skillet, heat oil. Make small patties from potato mixture (size and shape can suit your own needs). Place each patty into skillet; brown, turning once. Serve hot with any sauce, or wrap when cool for freezer.

Potato Skins

Slice partially cooled baked potatoes in half lengthwise; scoop out pulp (save pulp for use in sauces, soups, bread or Potato Cakes). Cut skins lengthwise again; place skin side down on baking sheet that has been sprayed with vegetable spray. Bake in 500°F (260°C) oven for about 10 minutes, until crisp.

Any of the following are great on the basic potato skin.

1. Sprinkle 1 tbsp (15 mL) of shredded low-fat old Cheddar and a sprinkle of granulated onion on the inside of each skin.

2. Sprinkle 1 to 2 tsp (5 mL to 10 mL) grated Parmesan cheese and ½ tsp (2 mL) fresh or dried chives on the inside of each skin.

3. Top the inside of each skin with chopped tomato, dried basil and shredded skim-milk mozzarella cheese.

Bake skins until they are almost done; add topping of choice. Continue to bake until they are browned. Serve hot.

Spinach

Look for the crispest, greenest leaf. It is best to buy spinach in an unpackaged bundle, as the packaged type usually has a lot of stems and bruised leaves. Avoid all spinach that is yellowing or that has a sour smell.

Frozen spinach is a fast alternative, and reliable when fresh is not really fresh. Frozen can be used in most recipes.

2 to 3 lb (1 kg to 1.5 kg) fresh spinach = 2 cups (500 mL) cooked

Remove stems and any yellowing or bruised leaves. Wash well in cold water.

With some recipes, the spinach will be added raw and cook along with the other ingredients. If a recipe calls for precooked spinach, blanch it: plunge spinach into boiling water to wilt it, then immediately rinse under cold water to stop the cooking. Spinach salads are at their best with only the freshest spinach. Spinach salads are found in the Salads chapter.

Spaghetti Squash

Look for a squash with a bright yellow skin that is hard and thick. It should feel heavy for its size. The average squash weighs 3 to 4 lbs (1.5 to 2 kg), and about ½ lb (250 g) will serve one person. Store the whole squash unwrapped at room temperature for up to 2 months.

Rinse outer shell; do not peel.

To bake: Pierce shell in several places; bake in 350°F (180°C) oven for 1 hour and 15 minutes, turning once during baking. Squash is ready when shell gives to pressure.

To microwave: Cut squash in half lengthwise; remove seeds. Place squash cut side up in microwave-safe baking dish. Cover and microwave on High for 12 to 14 minutes. Let stand, covered, for 5 minutes. The shell should give to pressure.

Use fork to pull spaghetti-like strands from shell.

Spaghetti squash may be used in place of pasta for a low-calorie alternative; try it with any of your favorite sauces. Toss cooked squash with 1 to 2 tbsp (15 mL to 25 mL) extra virgin olive oil; add your favorite herbs and grated Parmesan cheese. Small chopped and cooked vegetables may also be added.

Tomatoes

There are many varieties, shapes and sizes of tomato. As a general rule, select only firm (not like a baseball), unblemished ones with a deep red color. In season, this is easier to obtain; the tomato will taste according to the color and ripening time it had on the vine. When the markets are distant, the tomato gets picked green, so the vine-ripened flavor never develops.

Tip:
To improve the flavor (and ripening) of out-of-season tomatoes, place in a paper (not plastic) bag at room temperature for several days.

When a fresh tomato is at its ripest (locally grown), it requires little or no preparation aside from a light sprinkling of pepper or basil or other herbs, dried or fresh.

Skin and seeds can be removed before cooking, or in the case of puréed and sieved tomatoes, the skin and seeds can be left on before cooking. Opinions vary about the use of the seeds and skin in tomato sauces.

To peel a tomato, immerse for 30 seconds in a pot of boiling water; rinse under cold water. This will loosen the skin, making it easy to remove. Cut the tomato in two at the middle; scoop out the seeds with a very small spoon or melon baller. The tomato can then be chopped, cooked, sliced, added cold to salads, stuffed and otherwise dealt with in a variety of ways.

Canned stewed tomatoes are sometimes a better choice than poor-quality fresh ones for cooking and sauces. Read the label for any type of canned tomato product: salt is the usual additive, but sugar can also be present. Pure canned tomatoes, without salt and sugar, are available.

Baked Stuffed Tomatoes

The types of stuffings that can be used in a tomato are almost endless, from vegetables and pasta to meat, fish and poultry.

	Tomatoes (4 medium or 2 large)	
	Freshly ground pepper	
Half	pkg (10 oz/284 g) frozen chopped spinach, thawed and drained	Half
1	large clove garlic, minced (or 1 tsp/5 mL granulated)	1
1 tbsp	dried basil	15 mL
1 tbsp	dried parsley	15 mL
¼ tsp	dried thyme	1 mL
1 tbsp	olive oil	15 mL
1 cup	bread crumbs	250 mL
2	egg whites	2
3 tbsp	grated Parmesan cheese	50 mL

Wash tomatoes. Cut in half the large tomatoes or cut off just the very top of the medium tomatoes. Carefully scoop out and discard seeds and pulp. Sprinkle inside with freshly ground pepper; turn to drain on paper towel for 30 minutes.

Meanwhile, in large bowl, blend together remaining ingredients except Parmesan. Pack each drained tomato shell with stuffing. Arrange in shallow baking pan; sprinkle with Parmesan. Bake in 400°F (200°C) oven for 10 to 15 minutes; then place tomatoes under broiler until lightly browned. Makes 4 servings.

Baked Herbed Tomato Slices

4	tomatoes	4
¼ cup	grated Parmesan cheese	50 mL
1 tsp	dried basil	5 mL
1 tsp	granulated garlic	5 mL
1 tsp	dried parsley	5 mL
¼ tsp	freshly ground black pepper	1 mL

| 1 tsp | granulated onion | 5 mL |
| 2 tbsp | extra virgin olive oil | 25 mL |

Cut tomatoes into slices about ½ inch (1 cm) thick. Mix together remaining ingredients. In shallow baking dish, alternate layers of tomato and spicing mixture, ending with spicing mixture on top. Bake in 400°F (200°C) oven for 10 minutes; then place under broiler until lightly browned. Makes 4 to 5 servings.

Zucchini

Zucchini ranges in color; the most common variety sold is green. Look for small, firm, blemish-free zucchini that are heavy for their size. Avoid large zucchini, which tend to be bitter. Store in the refrigerator for up to 1 week, loosely wrapped.

1 lb (500 g) zucchini = 4 cups (1 L) grated
= 3½ cups (875 mL) sliced
3 zucchini = 1 lb (500 g) or 2 cups (500 mL) purée
1 zucchini = 2 cups (500 mL) sliced or 1½ cups (375 mL) shredded
2 zucchini = 2 cups (500 mL) diced

Very little needs to be done to this vegetable. Aside from washing and removing both ends, salting, which is a common practice to remove excess water, is not mandatory.

Zucchini Milk

Peel zucchini; cut into chunks. Place chunks in blender or food processor, blending until liquefied. Use this milk to replace dairy milk when baking yeast breads, quick breads, cakes, pancakes, muffins or waffles. It is also great in frozen desserts, casseroles, soups, stews, puddings and creamy pie fillings. Great for sauces, too. Freeze zucchini milk in recipe-size quantities, or in ice-cube trays for small quantities.

Steamed Zucchini

1 lb	zucchini (4 to 5 small), cut into ¼-inch (5 mm) slices	500 g

To microwave: steam zucchini in 8-cup (2 L) microwave-safe container on High for 4 to 6 minutes (no water is needed).

To sauté: In pan, sauté zucchini slices in their own juices until fork-tender (do not overcook).

After cooking, drain excess liquid from zucchini; mix in 1 tbsp (15 mL) lemon juice and 2 tsp (10 mL) dried parsley or 2 tbsp (25 mL) chopped fresh parsley. A small sprinkling of grated Parmesan is also nice.

Try 1 tbsp (15 mL) extra virgin olive oil mixed with 2 tbsp (25 mL) lime juice. Pour over steamed zucchini; lightly toss.

Grate unpeeled zucchini; sauté in small amount of stock or water to steam for about 3 minutes. Let cool; pack in freezer containers or bags. Add, without thawing, to soups or stews, vegetable sautés and omelets. Thaw and use in cakes, cookies, muffins and breads.

Potato-Zucchini Pudding

The combination of potato and zucchini is a natural, but try
the variations. This is a great way to use up small amounts of
fresh or leftover cooked vegetables, and it freezes well.

2 to 3 cups	coarsely grated zucchini	500 to 750 mL
3 to 4 cups	coarsely grated peeled potatoes	750 mL to 1 L
1	onion, chopped finely or puréed	1
2	egg whites	2
2 tbsp	sesame seed oil	25 mL
½ tsp	white pepper	2 mL
1 tsp	ground celery seed	5 mL
1 tsp	granulated garlic	5 mL
1 tsp	dry mustard	5 mL
½ cup	all-purpose flour	125 mL
1 tsp	baking powder	5 mL
¼ cup	grated Parmesan cheese (optional)	50 mL

In large bowl, mix together grated zucchini and potatoes. Add
remaining ingredients except Parmesan cheese. Mix well.
Pour mixture into 11- × 7-inch (2 L) glass baking dish.
Sprinkle with Parmesan cheese (if using). Bake in 350°F
(180°C) oven for 30 to 40 minutes until pudding has browned.
Makes 8 servings.

Variations:
Leftover cooked vegetables can be substituted for the
zucchini. Try the following: cauliflower, chopped green
beans, green peas, chopped broccoli. Other vegetable
combinations: thawed and drained spinach or fresh washed
and chopped; chopped sweet green or red peppers.

The Bread Basket

Bread Dough

There are many wonderful books written on the subject of bread making. It is an art that has had some renewed attention especially since new yeast products have been developed to cut the rising time in half. It is still a beautiful way to say "love" and "welcome home" to people you care about. The first step to making great bread is to know your ingredients.

Flour

All-purpose flour is made to be versatile to meet most baking needs; it can be used in bread dough, but it will not rise as high as a more glutenous flour. An easy way to find out the gluten content of flour is to check the protein range given in the nutritional information on the side of the package. If this protein information is not given, you can use the following as a guide. (Amounts of gluten [protein range] vary from brand to brand.)

Bread flour	12.5%
Unbleached flour	11%
All-purpose flour	9%
Pastry flour	8%
Cake flour	7% or less

Whole-wheat flour is not included in this list as it has a full quota of gluten, making it ideal to work with.

Rye has little gluten and must be mixed with a gluten flour to create the network for proper rising.

Other grains such as rice, corn, barley, buckwheat, oats and soy have good nutritional value, but should be mixed with a flour having a high gluten content, as these flours have little or none.

The unbleached flour sold in the U.S. has the closest affinity to the flour used by French bakers. If you cannot obtain this flour, a combination of three parts all-purpose to one part bread flour is a very close substitute. It is perfectly acceptable to use all-purpose flour in any of the recipes in this book.

Yeast and Other Leavenings

Yeast feeds on sugar and warmth to produce carbon dioxide to raise the dough and make it light. New yeast cultures have cut down the rising time by half. Two brands available are Fleischmann's RapidRise and Red Star's Quick-Rise. Take note that if you use these new yeasts, the temperature of the liquid added to the yeast is higher than with the older types of yeast — between 120°F and 130°F (49°C and 54°C) instead of the 100°F to 120°F (38°C to 49°C) tepid range. Use a kitchen thermometer to make sure the liquid is in the proper range according to the type of yeast being used.

When using yeast, all ingredients, except where otherwise stated, should be at room temperature. It is better to have the temperature on the cool side than overly hot. Hot will destroy yeast, cool will only retard its development.

Baking soda reacts with acids, sour cream, yogurt and buttermilk to produce carbon dioxide. It reacts almost instantly, requiring fast assembly and immediate baking.

Baking powder has a multiple action; the main release of gas comes from the heat of the oven.

Fats

Fat imparts richness and tenderness to bread. It also helps the gluten to rise. Many types of fats can be used, but for our purposes margarine or canola oil will be used. When a recipe calls for the fat to be melted, canola oil can be used instead of a solid fat. Using little or no fat will produce a dry and crisp bread, as in Italian or French.

Liquids

Milk makes a softer creamy white crumb and improves the nutrient value. Bread made with milk will not be as crusty as bread made without. For certain types of dough (depending on the use), a softer crust is more desirable.

Water produces that wonderful crusty bread that is so prized in French and Italian loaves, rye bread and crusty rolls.

The high lactic acid found in yogurt, buttermilk and sourdough starter works with yeast to create an excellent texture without the inconvenience of the usual rising, kneading and punching down routine. When using yogurt, buttermilk or sourdough, the first rising can be eliminated. The dough should be kneaded well to form the gluten network; then proceed directly to make the loaf. The dough is then allowed to rise before baking.

Tip:
Starting the dough-making process with an electric mixer (even better if you have dough hooks) will cut down on the time needed for conventional kneading. Beat well with about half of the called-for amount of flour. This will aid in developing the gluten.

Other liquids that can be used are limited only by your imagination. Try some of the following:

Yogurt
Fruit juices
Flat beer
Zucchini Milk (pg. 171)
Soup broths
Buttermilk
Vegetable juices
White wine
Cooking liquids
Potato water

Kneading and Rising
When dough is kneaded, gluten forms an elastic network to trap the carbon dioxide produced by the yeast. If the dough is sticky, add sprinkles of flour as needed. To determine if the

dough has enough flour, hit the dough with an open hand. If dough sticks to your hand, it needs more flour; if not, it is all right.

Follow the directions for kneading times in the recipes and do not be gentle with the dough. Use a push-turn-fold action and vent all your aggression; it will make terrific dough.

A stoneware bowl is ideal for raising the dough, though any bowl can be used. The bowl should be covered with plastic wrap to contain the moisture and keep the temperature more consistent. If the dough is placed in a plastic bag, make sure it is of sufficient size to allow the dough to expand. The dough should be placed in a warm, draft-free place to rise.

A gas oven having a lit pilot is an ideal location. An electric oven can also be used; heat the oven on the lowest setting for a few minutes to warm it, but be careful not to overwarm it. A convection oven can be set to the exact temperature needed. Or place a heating pad under the bowl with a thick towel between; set the pad on the lowest setting. Keep the bowl covered with plastic wrap.

Sweeteners
For our purposes, sugar is limited to the small amount that is needed to feed the yeast. This amount should not be of concern to diabetics, since it is usually limited to 1 to 2 tbsp (15 mL to 25 mL). To create a sweet dough, sweetener can come from additional sugar, juice concentrates or other sweeteners.

Eggs
Some recipes do not contain eggs. If you do not want to use whole eggs, be aware that substituting all whites will change the texture of the dough. Unless a large number of eggs is used, the use of 1 or 2 eggs for 2 loaves should not be a serious problem. Eggs must be at room temperature.

Salt
Bread dough can be made without salt, but salt does work a chemical action on the rising of the dough. The commercial breads on the market contain enormous amounts of salt; this is not needed for any other purpose than to give an inferior loaf some taste. For our purpose, the amount of salt is kept to a minimum — what is needed for the dough to properly rise.

Optional Additions for Flavor, Texture and Nutrition
Many things can be added to a basic dough recipe to change the flavor, texture and nutrition. I encourage you to experiment with your favorite ingredients. Along with each recipe, I have included variations.

In general, whole-wheat flour can be substituted to any proportion, due to its fine gluten content. It is quite acceptable to substitute small amounts of other (no-gluten) flours in a recipe containing 3 cups (750 mL) or more of flour (e.g., ½ cup/125 mL wheat germ, oat bran, etc. will not harm the gluten development of the dough).

The addition of nuts, cheese and seeds will boost the flavor and add nutrition. Just keep in mind that it will also change the sodium, fat and calorie content.

To increase the nutrition of any bread dough, add a half cake of puréed tofu per 2½ cups (625 mL) flour used.

Basic Refrigerator Yeast Dough

This recipe comes from a time when women baked their own bread at home, before bakeries were established, when sliced bread was unknown. Even at that time, women tried to find ways to cut down on the time-consuming aspect of bread making. This recipe was the beginning of greater freedom in the kitchen and is a good basic dough for many yeast recipes.

1 cup	lukewarm water	250 mL
2 tsp	granulated sugar	10 mL
3	pkg dry granular yeast	3
1½ cups	skim milk	375 mL
½ cup	margarine	125 mL
¼ cup	granulated sugar	50 mL
2	eggs, well beaten	2
9 cups	(approx) all-purpose flour	2.25 L

In large mixing bowl, combine water, 2 tsp (10 mL) sugar and yeast; let mixture stand for 3 to 4 minutes.

Scald milk in microwave oven or in top of double boiler.

Add margarine to milk. Stir in ¼ cup (50 mL) sugar until sugar and margarine are dissolved. Let cool to lukewarm. (To hasten cooling, stand container in a basin of cold water and ice; stir.)

Stir cooled milk mixture into dissolved yeast mixture. Stir in eggs.

Add about half of the flour, beating until mixture is smooth and elastic (a dough hook on the electric mixer may be used). Add remaining flour, a part at a time, working in with your hands. Turn out dough on greased surface; knead lightly until smooth, about 3 minutes. Place dough in greased bowl large enough for dough to double in bulk. Cover top of bowl with plastic wrap; secure it with elastic. Place bowl in refrigerator; dough can be stored this way for 1 week. As the days go by, you can remove portions to make many types of bread, rolls or fancy yeast cakes.

Dough must be allowed to rise in pan for 1 hour before baking. Follow baking times for fancy breads or bake plain loaf in 350°F (180°C) oven for about 25 minutes. Makes 4 bread loaves or fancy yeast breads.

Basic Yogurt Bread

This is about the simplest basic yeast dough to make, and very reliable. It has terrific flavor and texture, and can be the basis for many yeast recipes.

2 cups	warm water	500 mL
4 tsp	dry yeast	20 mL
2 tbsp	honey	25 mL
1 tsp	salt	5 mL
2 tbsp	canola oil	25 mL
1 cup	low-fat (1%) yogurt (at room temperature)	250 mL
2 tbsp	vegetable oil	25 mL
7 cups	(approx) all-purpose flour (or several combinations)	1.75 L

In a large bowl of an electric mixer, place water, yeast, honey, salt and canola oil. Stir to dissolve yeast; let stand for 2 minutes.

Blend yogurt and vegetable oil. Add to yeast mixture; beat to blend. (Never add to the yeast mixture any ingredient that is cold from the refrigerator.)

Beat in 3 to 3½ cups (750 mL to 875 mL) of the flour, for 3 to 4 minutes to develop gluten. Add another 3 cups (750 mL) of the flour, stirring with wooden spoon. Turn dough onto flat surface; knead. If dough is still sticky, add another ½ cup (125 mL) flour. Knead for 5 minutes until dough is smooth and satiny. No rising period is needed before forming the loaves. See NOTE below.

To make 2 loaves of bread, divide dough in half; knead each half for a few seconds; shape into loaf. Place into 2 loaf pans sprayed with vegetable spray. Cover with cloth; let rise in warm place for 1 hour or until doubled in bulk. Bake in 350°F (180°C) oven for 40 minutes; remove from pans and let cool on wire rack.

Note:
Lactic acid works with yeast to make a light loaf with an excellent texture without the inconvenience of the rising-

punching-down step. Use buttermilk, yogurt or sourdough starter.

Cinnamon Twists

Very fast to make and simple, but don't let that fool you — these cinnamon twists are winners.

¼ cup	warm water	50 mL
1	pkg (or 1 tbsp/15 mL) dry yeast	1
1 tbsp	granulated sugar	15 mL
1 cup	low-fat (1%) yogurt	250 mL
½ tsp	baking soda	2 mL
1	egg	1
½ tsp	salt	2 mL
3¼ cups	all-purpose flour	800 mL
2 tbsp	melted margarine	25 mL
1 to 2 tsp	cinnamon	5 to 10 mL
¼ cup	brown sugar	50 mL

In large bowl, combine water, yeast and sugar. Let dissolve, about 3 to 5 minutes. Mix together yogurt and baking soda; add to yeast mixture. Add egg and salt; blend. Add flour. Turn out onto lightly floured surface; knead lightly for a few minutes to form smooth ball. Cover with damp cloth and let dough stand for 5 minutes.

Roll out dough, ¼ inch (5 mm) thick, into 24- × 6-inch (60 cm × 15 cm) rectangle. Spread margarine over surface. Sprinkle with cinnamon and brown sugar. Bring two long sides of dough together; press top surface lightly to seal to bottom surface. Using sharp knife, cut dough into 24 strips, each 1 inch (2.5 cm) wide. Hold each strip at both ends and twist, forming spiral stick. Place twists, about 2 inches (5 cm) apart, on baking sheets sprayed with vegetable spray. Press both ends firmly and flatly on baking sheet.

Cover with damp cloth; let twists rise for 1 hour and 15

minutes or until doubled in bulk. Bake in 375°F (190°C) oven for 12 to 15 minutes.

Variations:

• Add 1 tbsp (15 mL) grated orange or lemon rind to yeast mixture before flour is added.
• After sprinkling dough with cinnamon and brown sugar, sprinkle with about ¼ cup (50 mL) mini chocolate chips.
• Instead of brown sugar, spread 3 to 4 tbsp (50 mL) apricot jam (slightly warmed to melt) over surface; sprinkle cinnamon on top.

Crisp Bread Sticks

Fast and simple, now you can have great restaurant-like crisp bread sticks at home. Make extra — they will go fast.

1	pkg (or 1 tbsp/15 mL) dry yeast	1
1 cup	warm water	250 mL
½ tsp	salt (or 1 tsp/5 mL granulated onion or granulated garlic)	2 mL
2 cups	(approx) all-purpose flour	500 mL
1 tbsp	sesame seed oil	15 mL
1	egg white (optional)	1

Mix yeast into water; stir to dissolve. Add salt. Let stand for 2 minutes.

Pour flour into large mixing bowl.

Stir oil into yeast; add to flour. Using wooden spoon, mix until dough forms. Turn dough out onto work surface and knead for 1 minute, adding a bit of flour if sticky. Place dough into greased bowl; let rise for 30 minutes or until almost double in bulk. Punch down dough. Pull off pieces of dough the size of a walnut. Roll into pencil-thin strips, about 8 inches (20 cm) long. Place sticks about 1 inch (2.5 cm) apart on ungreased baking sheet. The sticks can be left plain or brushed with egg white (if using) and rolled in seeds or herbs.

Do not let the sticks rise before baking. Bake in 450°F (230°C) oven for 10 to 12 minutes. Let cool on rack; don't store airtight.

Variations:

- Substitute whole-wheat flour for 1 cup (250 mL) of the all-purpose.
- Other flours can be substituted for ½ cup (125 mL) of the all-purpose flour. Try oat, rice, corn or rye flour.

Sourdough

There is much folklore about the origins of sourdough, but it is no longer considered a complicated and mysterious commodity. In fact, with modern refrigeration and freezers, we can keep a starter going for years. When you learn about the simplicity of sourdough and its many uses, you will find the older a batch gets, the better it is. Varieties of liquids will also produce richer flavors.

All starters require warmth in their formative stages. A starter should be used at least once every 2 weeks, and replenished each time. However, the starter can be kept in the refrigerator for long periods and in the freezer indefinitely. If the starter is kept in the refrigerator or freezer, let it return to room temperature and it will become active again. If it doesn't bounce back after the freezer, it may need help with a sprinkle of dry yeast. Bring the starter to room temperature, stir in the yeast and let it bubble before using.

After replenishing the starter, it should remain at room temperature for at least a day before returning it to the refrigerator for an extended storage time.

When replenishing any type of sourdough, the liquid being

used can be different than what was used originally. I like to add small amounts of liquid that comes from steaming vegetables in the microwave oven. Homemade soup broth is also very good. This will give your sourdough incredible depth and flavor. The flour can be varied as well.

Never let metal come in contact with the starter. Use a glass or plastic container, and mix with a plastic or wooden spoon.

Any yeast dough recipe can be turned into sourdough bread with the addition of sourdough starter. Nutritional value can also be increased in any bread recipe by replacing a portion of the flour with non-instant skim-milk powder or soya flour. Oatmeal and other grains can also be added. Tofu will create a high-protein bread.

The following are some different types of starters. Starter can be made without the addition of commercial yeast.

Starter #1 (Without Yeast)

| 2 cups | all-purpose flour | 500 mL |
| 2 cups | skim milk | 500 mL |

Leave milk in warm place for 24 hours; then stir in flour. Let mixture sit in warm place until it bubbles. The starter can be left for 2 or 3 days to develop flavor, but should stand for at least 24 hours. Store in covered glass or plastic container.

To replenish: Add 1 cup (250 mL) milk and 1 cup (250 mL) flour; let stand at room temperature for at least 24 hours before returning it to refrigerator for longer storage.

Starter #2 (With Yeast)

2 cups	all-purpose flour	500 mL
2 cups	tepid water	500 mL
1	pkg (or 1 tbsp/15 mL) dry yeast	1

In plastic or glass container, stir all ingredients together. Let stand in warm, draft-free place for 24 hours.

To replenish: Add 1 cup (250 mL) liquid (any type) and 1 cup (250 mL) flour (any type).

Starter #3 (Without Yeast)

You can replace potato water with 2 cups (500 mL) hot water mixed with ½ cup (125 mL) potato flakes.

2 cups	warm potato water (left after boiling potato)	500 mL
2 cups	all-purpose flour	500 mL

In plastic or glass container, stir all ingredients together. Let stand in warm, draft-free place for 24 hours.

To replenish: see Starter #2.

Starter #4 (Without Yeast)

1 cup	warm water	250 mL
1¼ cups	all-purpose flour	300 mL
1 tsp	sugar	5 mL
1	potato, peeled and grated	1

In 4-cup (1 L) container (to allow for expansion) mix all ingredients together; place cloth over top. Let stand in warm place for 24 hours. Stir; cover tightly with plastic wrap. The mixture will become light and foamy in 2 or 3 days. Stir down each day. Pour fermented starter into container with tight lid; refrigerate. In 2 or 3 days, when a clear liquid collects on top, starter will be ripe and ready to use.

To replenish: see Starter #2.

Starter #5 (Without Yeast)

1 cup	skim milk	250 mL
3 tbsp	low-fat (1%) yogurt	50 mL
1 cup	all-purpose flour	250 mL

Warm milk to 90°F to 100°F (32°C to 38°C) in saucepan or microwave oven; remove from heat. Stir in yogurt. Pour into mixing bowl. Let stand for 8 to 24 hours. The starter should have consistency of yogurt. If liquid on top has turned a light pink, discard starter and start again. Gradually stir in flour until smooth; cover tightly. Let stand in warm place until mixture bubbles and has a sour smell, 2 to 5 days.

To replenish, stir in ½ cup (125 mL) skim milk and ½ cup (125 mL) all-purpose flour. Store in refrigerator, bringing it back to room temperature before using.

Sourdough Crescent Rolls

1 cup	sourdough starter (at room temperature)	250 mL
⅓ cup	canola oil	75 mL
1	egg, beaten	1
1 cup	(approx) flour	250 mL
½ tsp	baking powder	2 mL
1	egg white, beaten	1
1 tbsp	water	15 mL
	Sesame seeds (optional)	
	Poppy seeds (optional)	

Mix together sourdough starter, oil and egg. Add flour and baking powder.

Knead dough for a few minutes until smooth, adding more flour if needed. Roll into 9-inch (23 cm) circle. Cut into 16 wedges. Roll each piece, starting at wide edge, in to the point. Shape each roll into crescent; place on baking sheet sprayed with vegetable spray. Brush tops with egg white mixed with water. Sprinkle with sesame or poppy seeds, if desired. Bake in 400°F (200°C) oven for 10 minutes. Makes 16 rolls.

Easy Sourdough Bread

This dough can be used to make any shape loaf or rolls. One loaf of kneaded dough can be frozen; allow to come to room temperature and bake as directed.

2½ cups	warm water	625 mL
¼ cup	canola oil	50 mL
3 tbsp	granulated sugar	50 mL
3 cups	all-purpose flour	750 mL
1 cup	sourdough starter	250 mL
3½ cups	all-purpose flour	875 mL
1 tsp	baking powder	5 mL
1 tsp	baking soda	5 mL

Mix water, oil, sugar, 3 cups (750 mL) flour and sourdough starter; let stand in warm place for 4 to 6 hours.

Combine 3½ cups (875 mL) flour, baking powder and baking soda; add to sourdough mixture.

Knead dough until smooth, about 5 minutes or less. Shape into 2 loaves; place in loaf pans sprayed with vegetable spray. Bake in 375°F (190°C) oven for 35 minutes. Makes 2 loaves.

Basic Baking-Powder Biscuits

These biscuits are always a winner. Variety will make them everyone's favorite. Try them for breakfast, after school, or for a snack. This recipe may be doubled.

2 cups	all-purpose flour	500 mL
1 tbsp	baking powder	15 mL
¼ cup	margarine (cold)	50 mL
½ cup	low-fat (1%) yogurt	125 mL
⅔ cup	skim milk	150 mL

In large bowl use spoon to blend flour and baking powder. Cut margarine into flour, using two knives or fork or pastry cutter, until mixture resembles coarse meal. With a fork, mix in yogurt and milk until ball forms that separates from sides of bowl. Dough will be soft and slightly sticky. Turn onto lightly floured surface; flatten with your hand. Fold dough over 2 to 3 times. (This should be done gently; the secret to making good biscuits is not to overwork the dough.)

On lightly floured surface, pat dough into 1-inch (2.5 cm) thickness. Cut biscuits with water glass. Gently compact sides with your hands to make biscuit about 1½ inches (4 cm) high. Pat out and cut remaining dough.

Arrange close together on ungreased cookie sheet; bake in 450°F (230°C) oven for 12 to 15 minutes until golden on top. Makes about 8 large or 12 small biscuits.

Variations:
Add one of the following to the flour mixture before adding wet ingredients.

- Cheddar Biscuits: 2 oz (50 g) shredded low-fat old Cheddar and 1 tsp (5 mL) dry mustard
- Parmesan Biscuits: 2 oz (50 g) grated Parmesan cheese
- Raisin Biscuits: ⅓ cup (75 mL) raisins
- Lemon Biscuits: Reduce skim milk by ⅓ cup (75 mL) and add ⅓ cup (75 mL) lemon juice and 1 tbsp (15 mL) grated lemon rind.
- Blueberry Biscuits: 1 cup (250 mL) fresh or unsweetened frozen blueberries
- Cranberry Biscuits: 1 cup (250 mL) fresh or frozen cranberries; cut cranberries in half and sprinkle with 1 tbsp (15 mL) granulated sugar.
- Cheddar and Onion Biscuits: One onion, chopped and lightly browned, is great in combination with Cheddar cheese. A number of fresh or dried herbs can also be used alone or in numerous combinations.
- Cheddar and Herb Biscuits: 2 oz (50 g) shredded low-fat old Cheddar and 2 tbsp (25 mL) dried chives, dill or parsley (or ⅓ cup/75 mL fresh)
- Cheddar and Beer Biscuits: Replace skim milk with light

beer. Onion or herbs may also be used in this combination.

• Cottage Cheese Dill Biscuits: Reduce milk to ⅓ cup (75 mL). Reduce yogurt to ¼ cup (50 mL). Add ⅔ cup (150 mL) low-fat (1%) cottage cheese. Add 1 tbsp (15 mL) chopped fresh dill or 1 tsp (5 mL) dried dill.

• Apricot Biscuits: ½ cup (125 mL) chopped dried apricots

Notes:

The skim milk may be replaced by: water, fruit juice, soup broth, water from cooked potato, diet ginger ale, tomato soup or cooked puréed vegetables.

Any type of seeds can be sprinkled on top; brush top of dough with 1 egg white beaten with 2 tbsp (25 mL) water. Try any of the following seeds: poppy, sesame or caraway. Try toasted rolled oats or cornmeal (top and bottom). Mix some of them together for great combinations.

Basic Oat-Bran Baking-Powder Biscuits

This basic oat-bran biscuit can be varied by replacing the oat bran with another type of flour — whole-wheat, corn, rice, rye or soy. All the variations described after Basic Baking-Powder Biscuits work equally well.

2 cups	all-purpose flour	500 mL
1 cup	oat bran	250 mL
4½ tsp	baking powder	22 mL
6 tbsp	cold margarine	90 mL
¾ cup	low-fat (1%) yogurt	175 mL
¾ cup	skim milk or water	175 mL
1	egg white, beaten	1
	Toasted rolled oats or	
	sesame seeds	

In large bowl, mix flour, oat bran and baking powder; using pastry cutter or two knives, cut in margarine until mixture resembles coarse meal.

Add yogurt and milk; use fork to mix until ball forms that separates from side of bowl. Turn onto lightly floured surface; gently fold dough over 4 to 5 times, but do not overwork dough. Using your hand, pat dough to thickness of 1 inch (2.5 cm); cut biscuits with water glass. Brush top with egg white; sprinkle with toasted rolled oats. Bake on ungreased cookie sheet in 450°F (230°C) oven for 12 to 15 minutes until biscuits are browned. Makes 12 large or 16 small biscuits.

Traditional Bran Muffins

This is like the type we see in most commercial bakeries. It is dark with a rich bran flavor. The types of variations are almost endless. These muffins are sure to become a favorite.

2½ cups	all-bran cereal	625 mL
½ cup	skim milk	125 mL
1 cup	buttermilk	250 mL
1	egg	1
1 tbsp	vanilla	15 mL
3 tbsp	canola oil	50 mL
1 tbsp	molasses	15 mL
⅓ cup	brown sugar	75 mL
1 tbsp	instant coffee dissolved in 1 tbsp (15 mL) boiling water	15 mL
1 tbsp	unsweetened cocoa	15 mL
1 tbsp	brandy	15 mL
¼ tsp	ground ginger	1 mL
2 tbsp	baking powder	25 mL
1 tsp	baking soda	5 mL
1½ cups	all-purpose flour	375 mL

In small bowl, combine all-bran, skim milk and buttermilk; mix and set aside to let bran absorb the milk.

In large bowl, using wire whisk, beat egg with vanilla until light and frothy. Add oil, molasses, brown sugar, coffee dissolved in water, cocoa, brandy and ginger; beat for several minutes. Add soaked bran.

Mix baking powder and baking soda into all-purpose flour. Using a spatula, quickly fold flour mixture into wet ingredients. Stir to incorporate all the flour, but be careful not to overmix. Pour batter into a 12-cup muffin tin sprayed with vegetable spray. Bake in 375°F (190°C) oven for 30 minutes.

Variations:

- Raisin Bran: To wet ingredients before adding flour, mix in ⅓ to ½ cup (75 mL to 125 mL) raisins. The raisins may be replaced by chopped dried apricots, pears or pitted prunes. Combinations of these may also be used. A sprinkling of slivered almonds on top is also nice.
- Bran-Banana Chunk: To wet ingredients before adding flour, mix in 1 large or 2 small ripe bananas that have been chopped into ½-inch (1 cm) chunks.
- Bran-Apple Chunk: To wet ingredients before adding flour, mix in 1 large or 2 small washed apples (with skin) that have been chopped into ½-inch (1 cm) chunks. and mixed with ½ tsp (2 mL) cinnamon.
- Almond Bran: Add 1 tsp (5 mL) almond flavoring to basic wet ingredients. In small, dry pan, lightly brown ⅓ cup (75 mL) slivered almonds. Add almonds to flour mixture.

Note:
The almonds may be replaced with raw sunflower or pumpkin seeds (or a mixture). Brown them in a dry pan for a nuttier, more intense flavor. Omit almond flavor and use this combination of nuts with basic muffin or any variations.

- Orange or Lemon Bran: Replace instant coffee and water with 2 tbsp (25 mL) frozen lemon or orange juice concentrate that has been thawed. Add 1 tsp (5 mL) grated lemon or orange rind. These flavors can be combined with other variations.
- Blueberry Bran: Replace brandy with 1 tbsp (15 mL) white

rum. Replace instant coffee and water with 2 tbsp (25 mL) frozen lemon juice concentrate that has been thawed. To flour mixture add 1 cup (250 mL) fresh or frozen unsweetened blueberries. Mix to coat with flour and distribute.

• Chocolate Chip — White Chocolate Chip: To flour before adding wet ingredients, mix in ⅓ cup (75 mL) of your favorite type of chips: chocolate butterscotch, white, milk chocolate, etc.

Classic Banana Bread

Eating this is almost like taking a trip to Jamaica, where some of the best banana bread comes from. This recipe can have some variations that work well with the basic magnificent flavor. When the bread is cool, I slice it in ½-inch (1 cm) pieces and freeze in a plastic bag. I can remove as much as I need and thaw it in the microwave oven or toaster oven.

1¾ cups	all-purpose flour	425 mL
1 tbsp	baking powder	15 mL
¼ cup	margarine (at room temperature)	50 mL
½ cup	brown sugar	125 mL
1	egg	1
1 tsp	grated orange rind	5 mL
1 tbsp	orange juice concentrate, thawed	15 mL
1 tbsp	dark rum	15 mL
1 tsp	coconut extract or almond extract	5 mL
2	very ripe large bananas, mashed	2
⅓ cup	golden raisins (optional)	75 mL
½ cup	low-fat (1%) yogurt	125 mL
½ tsp	baking soda	2 mL

Mix together flour and baking powder; set aside.

In large bowl of electric mixer, cream together margarine and brown sugar. Add egg, continuing to beat for 2 minutes until mixture is light and fluffy. Add orange rind as mixture continues to beat.

While beating, add orange juice concentrate, dark rum, coconut extract. Add mashed bananas, beating for 1 minute.

Using spatula, mix in raisins (if using). Combine yogurt with baking soda. When yogurt foams up to double its volume, pour flour mixture, then yogurt into wet ingredients, using spatula to mix well. Batter should be well mixed.

Pour into loaf pan that has been sprayed with vegetable spray. Bake in 375°F (190 °C) oven for about 1 hour.

When done, let stand in pan on rack for 5 minutes; remove from pan and let cool on rack. Makes 1 loaf.

Variations:

The addition of raisins, chopped dried apricots, apples or peaches, dates and nuts works very well. Even small amounts combined create a nice blend with the banana.

- Chocolate Banana Bread: To the basic creamed mixture, add ¼ cup (50 mL) unsweetened cocoa powder. Nuts and/or white chocolate chips may also be used. Dried apricots work well in this combination.
- Banana Cranberry or Blueberry Bread: To flour mixture, add ½ to ¾ cup (125 mL to 175 mL) cranberries or blueberries; mix well to coat and distribute.

Favorite Pastas and Grains

Homemade Pasta

Homemade pasta is superior to the store-bought dried varieties. (In all fairness, some dried packaged varieties have improved in recent years.) I will confess that I rarely ever make my own pasta, because of the time involved. Most supermarkets now carry good fresh varieties. If you do have the time, the following recipe is for a very good pasta that is not commercially available.

Note:
If you are going to make pasta regularly, consider investing in a simple pasta machine, for rolling by hand is a very hard job.

Corn Noodles

This pasta dough recipe can be used to prepare any size or shape of noodles. It makes great lasagna with cheese or meat.

1 cup	corn flour	250 mL
1½ cups	all-purpose flour	375 mL
2	eggs (or 1 whole egg + 2 whites)	2
1 tbsp	olive oil	15 mL
3 to 4 tbsp	warm water	50 mL

In large bowl, mix together corn flour and all-purpose flour. In separate bowl, beat together eggs, oil and water. Pour wet into dry ingredients and mix. Add extra water if needed. The dough will be hard but requires some kneading by hand.

Break off a piece of dough. Using #3 setting on pasta machine, process dough through machine several times until dough is desired thickness and texture.

Set machine to desired noodle cut. Hang cut noodles to air dry. Noodles can be cooked immediately, refrigerated, tightly wrapped, for several days, or frozen.

Any sauce may be used. Corn noodles are great served with spicy chili and steamed green vegetables.

Pressed Herb Noodles

This is a super-fast way of making wonderful herb noodles if you do not have a pasta machine. (If you have one it may be used.) Or you can substitute homemade pasta dough for the egg roll wrappers. Serve as a side dish with 1 to 2 tbsp (15 to 25 mL) extra virgin olive oil, granulated garlic and grated Parmesan cheese. Or bake noodles for 15 minutes at 350°F (180°C) with low-fat cottage cheese, garlic and grated Parmesan cheese.

2	pkg egg roll wrappers	2
	Fresh herbs	

Brush 4 to 6 egg roll wrappers with water. Lay 3 or 4 herb leaves on one half of each wrapper. Fold the other half over the herb leaves. Roll each wrapper several times lengthwise with a rolling pin until dough is thin and sealed. (Or put through a pasta machine several times.)

Cut each rolled wrapper into noodles of desired width. Hang to air dry. Cook, or refrigerate or freeze.

Variation:
Use corn dough to make Herb Corn Noodles.

Cheese-Noodle Pudding with Fruit

This pudding makes a great light dinner when served with a green salad. It can be eaten hot or cold.

1	pkg (14 to 16 oz/500 g) medium-width egg noodles	1
2	egg whites	2
½ cup	brown sugar	125 mL
1 tbsp	cinnamon	15 mL
1 tsp	vanilla	5 mL
2 tbsp	brandy	25 mL
16 oz	low-fat (1%) cottage cheese	500 g
1	can (19 oz/540 mL) unsweetened crushed pineapple, drained	1
¼ cup	all-purpose flour	50 mL

Boil noodles according to package directions until al dente; rinse and drain.

In large bowl, beat egg whites until frothy; stir in brown sugar, cinnamon, vanilla, brandy and cottage cheese. Add crushed pineapple and flour; mix. Pour mixture over noodles, blending and folding together.

Pour into 11- × 7-inch (2 L) glass baking dish sprayed with vegetable spray. Sprinkle with extra cinnamon. Bake in 350°F (180°C) oven for 45 minutes or until browned. Makes 6 to 8 servings.

When cooled, this pudding can be cut into serving-size pieces and wrapped in waxed paper, then stored in a freezer plastic bag for several months.

Variations:

• Substitute for the pineapple 2 grated apples (with skin off or on).
• Substitute for the pineapple 3 large or 4 small peaches: peel, remove pit and chop. Unsweetened canned peaches substitute well for the fresh. Mix 1½ tsp (7 mL) cinnamon into cottage cheese; adjust to taste.

• A number of other fruits may be substituted. Use fresh fruit unless the canned fruit is packed in its own juice with no sugar added. Try mashed bananas, oranges, plums, blueberries, cranberry-apple, ½ cup (125 mL) raisins.

Stuffed Manicotti

Manicotti shells may be purchased in the store, but by the time they are cooked and drained, they are very hard to handle, and this method is very time-consuming. Some stores now carry a new type that do not have to be precooked. These are better, but still difficult and time-consuming to stuff. The fastest and easiest method I have ever found is to buy a package of premade egg roll wrappers and roll them up with the filling inside. There is no precooking, and they bake quickly in the oven. Both recipes for cheese- and meat-stuffed manicotti are presented here.

1	pkg egg roll wrappers	1
1 cup	shredded skim-milk mozzarella cheese	250 mL

Cheese Filling:

16 oz	low-fat (1%) cottage cheese	500 g
Half	pkg (10 oz/284 g) frozen chopped spinach, thawed and drained	Half
1	egg (or 2 egg whites)	1
3 tbsp	all-purpose flour	50 mL
2 tsp	granulated garlic	10 mL
2 tsp	granulated onion	10 mL

Sauce:

1½ to 2 cups	tomato sauce	375 to 500 mL
¼ cup	dry white wine	50 mL
2 tbsp	Italian herbs	25 mL
1 tbsp	granulated onion	15 mL

1 tbsp	granulated garlic	15 mL
1 tbsp	dried basil	15 mL
1 tbsp	chili powder	15 mL

To make cheese stuffing:
In small bowl, mix together all ingredients.

Remove one egg roll wrapper at a time from package. Lay it flat, with one edge facing you. Place about ¼ cup (50 mL) filling in line across dough, about 1½ inches (4 cm) from bottom edge.

Fold the bottom edge over filling; roll. Place stuffed manicotti, seam side down, in baking dish. Do not crowd manicotti; leave about ¼ inch (5 mm) between them to allow for growth in baking. Use up filling and egg roll covers.

To make sauce:
Combine tomato sauce, wine, Italian herbs, onion, garlic, basil and chili powder; pour over manicotti.

Bake, covered, in 350°F (180°C) oven for 25 minutes. Remove cover; sprinkle with mozzarella. Bake, uncovered, for 5 minutes, just to melt cheese. Makes 4 to 5 servings.

Meat Stuffing:

1½ lb	extra-lean ground beef, veal or chicken	800 g
2	small or 1 large ripe tomato, chopped	2
1	onion, finely chopped	1
1 tbsp	granulated garlic	15 mL
1 tbsp	Italian spices	15 mL
1 tbsp	dried tarragon	15 mL
¼ cup	dry red or white wine	50 mL

Place all ingredients in skillet; cook until meat is browned. Follow method above for assembling manicotti.

Angel Hair Pasta and Meatballs

This classic spaghetti-and-meatball dish can be updated with variations. It can even become a totally vegetarian dish if you omit the meatballs and use the variations in any number of combinations. I like to use the angel hair pasta, but any spaghetti noodle may be used. To speed the assembly of this dish, frozen meatballs can be used, ready to heat in the sauce. Meatballs can be beef, veal, chicken or any combination as long as the meat is extra lean.

Pasta
Meatballs
Grated Parmesan cheese

Sauce:

1	can (13 oz/369 mL) tomato paste (no salt added)	1
3 cups	water	750 mL
¼ cup	dry white wine	50 mL
2 tbsp	granulated onion	25 mL
2 tbsp	granulated garlic	25 mL
3 tbsp	Italian herbs	50 mL
2 tbsp	chili powder	25 mL
½ tsp	freshly ground green peppercorns	2 mL
1 tbsp	extra virgin olive oil	15 mL

To make sauce:
In 12-cup (3 L) pot, mix all ingredients except olive oil. Cook gently over medium-low heat for 5 minutes.

Add meatballs to sauce; cook for 5 minutes (if frozen, gently heat until thawed). Stir in olive oil after sauce has cooked.

Follow package directions for cooking pasta; the pasta should be al dente. Drain and rinse. Serve sauce and meatballs on side. Serve grated Parmesan cheese at the table. Makes 6 servings.

Variations:
Add any one or a number of the following to sauce after
meatballs are heated. Take care not to overcook vegetables.

> 1 cup (250 mL) cut-up broccoli
> ½ cup (125 mL) small whole mushrooms
> ½ cup (125 mL) snow peas
> ½ cup (125 mL) green beans, cut to bite size
> 1 cup (250 mL) small brussels sprouts

Note:
For a change, chop up any leftover cooked meat, chicken or
fish; add to sauce. Cooked chunks of stewing meat can also
be substituted for the meatballs. Mixtures of lean meats in
this sauce add to its flavor.

Skinny Baked Lasagna

Lasagna is among the more popular American-Italian dishes.
With the new oven-ready and fresh-made noodles, this dish
has become a fast oven-to-table dinner. This recipe cuts down
on the extra pasta to trim down the calories, although the
spinach layers may be replaced with the usual noodles and the
spinach (chopped frozen type) mixed into the cheese or meat
filling.

1	recipe tomato sauce (see Angel Hair Pasta and Meatballs, pg. 199)	1
6	oven-ready lasagna noodles	6
2	16 oz (500 g) containers low-fat (1%) cottage cheese	2
1	egg	1
1 tbsp	dried parsley (or 2 tbsp/25 mL fresh chopped)	15 mL
2 tbsp	dried Italian herbs	25 mL
4 tbsp	all-purpose flour	50 mL

1 tbsp	granulated garlic	15 mL
1	bunch fresh spinach	1
1	large tomato, sliced thin	1
4 tbsp	grated Parmesan cheese	50 mL
¼ cup	water or dry white wine	75 mL
1 cup	shredded skim-milk mozzarella cheese	250 mL

Pour enough tomato sauce into a 13- by 9-inch (3.5 L) baking dish to cover bottom. Place 3 noodles side by side over sauce; noodles should not touch.

In medium bowl, mix together cottage cheese, egg, parsley, Italian herbs, flour and garlic.

Remove stems from spinach; wash and dry leaves. Set aside.

Spread about ½ cup (125 mL) cottage-cheese mixture over lasagna noodles in pan. Cover with spinach leaves. Repeat with remaining cheese mixture and spinach. End with remaining 3 lasagna noodles. Pour remaining sauce carefully over noodles and into sides of baking dish. Cover with tomato slices. Sprinkle with Parmesan cheese. Carefully pour ¼ cup (75 mL) water or dry white wine into baking dish. Cover with foil (shiny side up) and bake at 350°F (180°C) for 20 minutes. Remove foil. Check that pan has lots of sauce; if not, gently pour in extra water or white wine, carefully blending it into sauce with a small spoon. Sprinkle with mozzarella, turn off heat and return dish to oven, uncovered, for 10 minutes to melt cheese. Serve hot. Makes 6 to 8 servings.

Variations:
Substitute 2 lb (1 kg) extra-lean ground beef, chicken or veal for the cottage cheese. Omit the egg. Half a 10-oz (284 g) package frozen spinach, thawed and lightly drained, may be mixed into the meat, and extra pasta noodles may be used between layers.

Any favorite pasta sauce may be used. Try some of the sauces in "All Sauced Up and Everywhere to Go".

Macaroni and Turkey Casserole

Extra-lean ground turkey is used in this recipe, although it is just as tasty with extra-lean ground chicken.

1	onion, finely chopped	1
1 lb	extra-lean ground turkey	500 g
1 tbsp	all-purpose flour	15 mL
2 cups	uncooked macaroni	500 mL
½ lb	fresh mushrooms, thickly sliced	250 g
1 tbsp	dried Italian herbs	15 mL
1 tbsp	dried tarragon	15 mL
1 tbsp	granulated garlic	15 mL
1 tbsp	chili powder	15 mL
5 cups	low-sodium tomato juice	1.25 L
2 tbsp	Worcestershire sauce	25 mL
2 tbsp	grated Parmesan cheese	25 mL

In non-stick skillet sprayed with vegetable spray, brown onion. Add turkey. Sprinkle meat with flour; brown. Pour mixture into 4-quart (4 L) stove-top casserole. Stir in uncooked macaroni, mushrooms, herbs and spices. Add tomato juice and Worcestershire sauce; blend well. Simmer, covered, over low heat 12 to 15 minutes until macaroni is tender and liquid is absorbed. Sprinkle with Parmesan cheese. Makes 4 to 5 servings.

Buckwheat with Bow Ties and Peas

This is a terrific accompaniment to just about any meat or poultry dish.

1 tbsp	virgin olive oil	15 mL
1	onion, finely chopped	1
1 cup	toasted whole buckwheat groats (kasha)	250 mL
1	egg white	1
1½ cups	chicken stock (or 3 tbsp/50 mL low-sodium chicken	375 mL

	soup powder dissolved in 1½ cups/375 mL water)	
	Freshly ground black pepper	
2 tsp	granulated garlic	10 mL
2 tsp	granulated onion	10 mL
1½ tsp	Season All	7 mL
¾ cup	small bow tie pasta (uncooked)	175 mL
½ cup	frozen green peas	125 mL

Heat olive oil in non-stick pan. Sauté onion for 5 minutes until browned.

In bowl, combine buckwheat with egg white; mix to coat well. Pour into pan; cook over high heat until mixture is dry. Add chicken stock, pepper, garlic, onion and Season All; reduce heat to low. Simmer until most of the liquid is absorbed.

Meanwhile, drop bow ties into a pot of boiling water. Test pasta after they have cooked for 1 minute. When pasta is al dente, drain and rinse.

Just before liquid is absorbed from kasha, add frozen peas; cook until remaining liquid is absorbed. Add bow ties to buckwheat; mix gently. Serve hot. Serves 6 as a side dish.

Variations:

• Omit green peas and use chopped sautéed sweet green or red pepper, or chopped spinach.
• Omit green peas and add 1 to 2 grated carrots; add 4 chopped mushrooms almost at the end of cooking.

Orzo or Bulgar with Mushrooms and Greens

Orzo is a rice-shaped pasta — very versatile and ready to stand in for rice. In this recipe, the orzo can be replaced with bulgar, or try it with brown rice.

1 tbsp	virgin olive oil	15 mL
1 cup	orzo	250 mL
3 tbsp	low-sodium chicken soup powder	50 mL
2 cups	water	500 mL
2	cloves garlic, finely chopped (or 1 tbsp/15 mL granulated)	2
1 tbsp	granulated onion	15 mL
1 tsp	dried thyme	5 mL
	Freshly ground pepper	
½ lb	mushrooms	250 g

One of the following:

½ cup	green peas	125 mL
Half	pkg (10 oz/284 g) frozen chopped spinach	Half
½ cup	french-style green beans	125 mL
½ cup	chopped green beans	125 mL
½ cup	finely chopped celery, sautéed	125 mL

In large skillet, place olive oil and orzo; cook over medium heat for 5 minutes. Stir frequently to brown.

Dissolve soup powder in water; add to orzo. Sir in garlic, onion, thyme and pepper; cook until orzo has absorbed most of the liquid, about 10 minutes. Add mushrooms and green vegetable of choice; continue to cook until orzo is tender but still moist. Serve hot as a side dish. Serves 4 to 5.

Farfel

Farfel can be commercially bought, but is not available everywhere. It is in the pasta family, since the dough is exactly the same, but it is the preparation that separates it. If you have the time, Homemade Farfel (pg. 206) is worth the effort, and it can be made in large quantities.

1	pkg (7 oz/210 g) commercially prepared farfel or 1 cup (250 mL) homemade farfel	1
2¹/₄ cups	water	550 mL
1 tbsp	granulated onion (or 1 small onion, finely chopped and lightly sautéed with olive oil spray)	15 mL
2 tbsp	low-sodium chicken soup powder	25 mL
2 tbsp	low-sodium beef soup powder	25 mL
1 tsp	granulated garlic	5 mL
2 tsp	Season All	10 mL
3 tbsp	dry white wine (optional)	50 mL
¹/₄ tsp	ground white or green peppercorns	1 mL

In oven-proof baking dish with lid, combine all ingredients.

Bake, covered, in 350°F (180°C) oven until all liquid is absorbed, or cook in microwave oven at Medium-High for 10 to 12 minutes. The farfel can also be cooked on top of stove until moisture is absorbed. Spices can be adjusted to taste (2 tbsp/25 mL gravy from fat-free chicken, turkey or beef can be added when farfel is cooked). Makes 4 to 5 side servings.

Note:

My mother used to cook farfel in the oven when she had a roast or chicken cooking. Several spoonfuls of the gravy from the meat would be added at the end of cooking. I have vivid memories of the old ceramic baked bean dish that she cooked it in. It seemed to give it a deep rich baked flavor. Several years ago, I found a similar old ceramic baker; it may be my memories, but I like the farfel cooked in this dish.

Variations:
Ten minutes before farfel has completed cooking in oven or after 10 minutes of cooking in microwave, some of the following may be added.

> ½ cup (125 mL) frozen green peas
> ½ cup (125 mL) sliced mushrooms
> ½ cup (125 mL) chopped broccoli

As well, ½ cup (125 mL) any leftover cooked vegetable may be added almost at end of cooking time.

Homemade Farfel

Farfel can be made in quantity, but it must be stored in the refrigerator until it is used, as it has no preservatives.

3	eggs (or 1 whole egg + 3 whites)	3
¼ cup	(approx) water	50 mL
2½ cups	all-purpose flour	625 mL

Beat eggs with water. Add flour; mix to create very stiff dough. Divide in half; wrap each half in plastic wrap. Place dough in freezer for 1 hour or more. This makes it easier to grate.

Grate dough on coarse grater; spread gratings (farfel) on large cookie sheet. Bake in 300°F (150°C) oven to dry and brown. It will be necessary to turn and move farfel to ensure even drying and browning. When done, remove from oven and let cool. Refrigerate in airtight container. Homemade farfel will keep for 2 months. Use in place of commercially prepared farfel.

Corn Farfel

1 cup	corn flour	250 mL
1½ cups	all-purpose flour	375 mL
3	eggs (or 1 whole egg + 3 whites)	3
¼ cup	(approx) warm water	50 mL

Mix two flours together; then proceed as for Homemade Farfel.

Oatmeal

Oatmeal in North America was for many years thought of as just a breakfast cereal. The recent oat-bran and oatmeal craze came about with new information to support its renewed use for its fiber and vitamins in a well-balanced diet.

Whole-grain oats are nutritionally important, containing seven B vitamins and vitamin E. Oats also supply us with nine minerals. Oats contain important insoluble fiber to regulate digestive functions. They also contain soluble fibers that assist in controlling blood sugar elevations and lower blood-cholesterol levels. The bran portion of the oat kernel (called a grout), which remains after the hull is removed, is a concentrated source of soluble fiber.

There have been so many claims made in the last few years about the benefits of eating oat bran, and food processors have really jumped to the front in using this almost forgotten grain. We can be sure of two things: oats are nutritionally good for us and it is of benefit to include this grain in a well-balanced food plan. However, does a small amount of oat bran added to a highly processed food item afford us any real benefit? It would seem that including oats in our everyday cooking would be a far more sensible and beneficial approach to the oat-bran frenzy.

Oats can be bought in many forms — whole rolled oats, quick-cooking instant, oat bran, oat flour and oat groats. No matter which form of oats you purchase, they all contain three elements:

- the germ: a source of vitamins, minerals and protein
- the endosperm: contains protein and carbohydrates and is a good source of energy
- the bran: one of the best sources of fiber

Throughout this book, you will find many recipes using oatmeal. There are many ways to add this wholesome grain to our diet as well as enjoy its versatile flavor.

Know Your Oats

- Old-fashioned Rolled Oats (5-minute oats). These are large separate flakes produced from the whole groat. They are steamed and rolled flat.
- Quick-Cooking Oats (1-minute oats). These are rolled oats that have been cut into small pieces and heat-treated for faster cooking.
- Oat Flour. This can be store-bought or homemade. Regular oatmeal is ground to a very fine flour consistency. The flour can be used for baking, as a thickening agent, and as a replacement for people with wheat allergy.
- Oat Bran. This finely ground flour type of product is made from only the outer layer of the whole oat. Oat bran is used in many products because of its high fiber content. It can be added to many recipes as a nutrient supplement.

Using Oat Flour

To make whole grain oat flour, place a quantity of uncooked rolled oats in a blender. Blend for 1 minute or until oats are powdered. Roughly 1¼ cups (300 mL) oats will make 1 cup (250 mL) oat flour. A large quantity can be made and stored in a covered container, lasting for about 6 months (with no need for refrigeration).

In most recipes, you can replace up to but no more than one-third of the all-purpose flour called for. Ground oat flour lacks the gluten found in all-purpose flour, but proper proportions of all-purpose flour and oat flour will create a firm structure with a richer taste and a more tender texture.

Another use for oat flour is as a soothing oatmeal bath. Place about ⅓ cup (75 mL) oatmeal flour into the toe of an old stocking. Add some dried rosemary, thyme and orange peel (optional); knot the stocking, containing the ingredients tightly. Place this into the bath when running the water. Most of it will dissolve; this is very soothing for skin irritations, and is relaxing for tired muscles. The plain oatmeal works well for children and babies with rashes or chicken pox.

Using Toasted Oats

Toasting gives oatmeal a rich brown color and a nutty taste, along with a slightly crunchy texture. Toasted large-flake oats are a terrific substitute for nuts or as a crunchy topping in any recipe. Process them in a blender and substitute them for bread crumbs.

To toast oats place up to 3 cups (750 mL) large-flake uncooked oats in a shallow ungreased jelly-roll pan or baking dish. Toast in 350°F (180°C) oven for 12 to 15 minutes or until golden brown. Let cool. Store in a closed container for up to 6 months without refrigeration. Again, a larger quantity may be made.

Browned oatmeal with ground browned almonds makes a crunchy topping for desserts — both baked and unbaked types. Great with frozen yogurt.

Golden Oats (Basic)

Golden oats are a more nourishing substitute for rice or noodles. They can be served as a side dish or under stew or with any saucy meat dish.

To 1½ cups (375 mL) uncooked large-flake oats, mix in 1 well-beaten egg (or 2 well-beaten egg whites) until oats are thoroughly coated.

Place 1 tbsp (15 mL) canola oil in a heated skillet; add oat mixture. Cook over medium heat until lightly browned. The golden oats can be stored in a covered container in the refrigerator for several weeks, or frozen for long-term storage.

1½ cups	Golden Oats	375 mL
¾ cup	water	175 mL
1 tbsp	low-sodium chicken soup powder	15 mL
1 tbsp	low-sodium beef soup powder	15 mL
1 tbsp	granulated onion	15 mL
¼ tsp	white pepper	1 mL
2 tsp	Season All	10 mL
1 tsp	dried sage	5 mL
1 cup	frozen green peas or corn	250 mL

Place Golden Oats in 8-cup (2 L) oven-proof casserole (or microwave-safe casserole). Combine water, chicken soup powder, beef soup powder, onion, pepper, Season All and sage; blend into oats. Cook until water is almost absorbed. Add green peas; continue cooking until all liquid is absorbed.

Instant Oatmeal For Breakfast

Packaged instant oatmeal contains large amounts of sodium and, in the case of flavored types, large amounts of sugar and chemicals are used to preserve the shelf life. Regular rolled oats in any form do not require chemicals for preserving. Being an almost perfect food, it comes with its own natural preservatives. For a very fast low-calorie high-fiber oatmeal breakfast that will get you through the morning, try the following.

½ cup	regular quick-cooking (1-minute) oats	125 mL
2 tbsp	instant skim-milk powder (or 1 tbsp/15 mL powdered buttermilk)	25 mL

Boil some water. Put oats in coffee mug. Pour ¾ cup (175 mL) boiling water into mug. Stir. Add milk powder; stir. Let oatmeal stand for 3 to 4 minutes.

Variations:

• The oatmeal is ready to eat, but if you would like, small amounts of chopped fruit may be added: banana, strawberries, apples, oranges, blueberries, raisins, kiwi, pineapple.
• For chocoholics: Add ½ tsp (2 mL) pure cocoa and 1 pkg sugar substitute.
• To improve nutrition, 1 tsp (5 mL) wheat germ can be added.
• A dash of cinnamon is terrific, especially with chopped apples.
• For those not concerned about sugar: small amounts of honey, maple syrup or brown sugar can be added to taste. Sweetened chocolate syrup or 1 tsp (5 mL) instant chocolate can also be added.
• For a nuttier flavor, use toasted oats instead of plain.

Heavenly Pies and Desserts

Baked Apples

This is an old favorite that just keeps coming back. There are many variations to this simple apple. Use 1 apple per person.

4	large Spy or other cooking apples	4
	Orange juice, pineapple juice, apple juice or sugar-free soda	
1	pkg (4-serving size) sugar-free gelatin	1
½ cup	water	125 mL
½ cup	instant skim-milk powder	125 mL
½ cup	water	125 mL
½ tsp	vanilla	2 mL
	Cinnamon	
1 tbsp	brown sugar	15 mL
	Sliced strawberries or blueberries	
¾ cup	apple juice	175 mL

Wash apples; remove core about ¾ of the way down. Place apples in oven-proof baking dish. Into each apple center pour orange juice.

Mix gelatin with ½ cup (125 mL) boiling water; stir until dissolved. Pour into apples, pouring any leftover into pan.

Mix skim-milk powder, ½ cup (125 mL) water and vanilla; pour into apples, pouring remainder into pan. Sprinkle apple tops with cinnamon and brown sugar.

Stuff center of each apple with sliced strawberries. Pour apple juice into apple centers, pouring extra into pan. Bake, covered, in 375°F (190°C) oven for about 30 minutes. Uncover; baste. Cook for 10 to 15 minutes longer.

(Microwave method: microwave in a microwave-safe dish, covered, for 8 to 10 minutes for 4 apples. Check time with manufacturer's recommendation for your oven.)

Makes 4 servings.

Oatmeal-Crunch Baked Apples

4 to 6	large Spy or other cooking apples	4 to 6
¾ cup	large-flake oatmeal	175 mL
⅓ cup	all-purpose flour	75 mL
1 tsp	cinnamon	5 mL
¼ cup	brown sugar or sugar substitute	50 mL
3 tbsp	canola oil	50 mL
½ cup	orange juice	125 mL
1 tbsp	brandy (or 2 tsp/10 mL brandy extract)	15 mL

Prepare apples as in Baked Apples (pg. 212); place in baking dish.

In small bowl, mix oatmeal, flour, cinnamon, sugar and oil. Pack mixture into center of each apple, sprinkling leftover mixture over apples. Stir together orange juice and brandy; pour into pan. Bake, covered, in 375°F (190°C) oven 20 minutes. Uncover; bake 10 minutes. Makes 4 to 6 servings.

Oatmeal-Apple Crisp

This is a lower-calorie and lower-sugar version of an old favorite.

5 to 6	large cooking apples, peeled, cored and sliced	5 to 6
2 tsp	cinnamon	10 mL
⅓ cup	brown sugar	75 mL
1 tbsp	lemon juice	15 mL
1 tbsp	cornstarch	15 mL
½ cup	orange juice	125 mL
2 tbsp	brandy (or 2 tsp/10 mL brandy extract)	25 mL

Topping:

1 cup	rolled oats	250 mL
½ cup	all-purpose flour	125 mL
1 tsp	cinnamon	5 mL
⅓ cup	brown sugar	75 mL
⅓ cup	margarine	75 mL

In large bowl, combine sliced apples with cinnamon, sugar, lemon juice, cornstarch, orange juice and brandy. Mix well to blend.

In small bowl, combine the topping ingredients. Mix well to blend.

Pour apples into oven-proof glass 11- × 7-inch (2 L) baking dish. Sprinkle topping evenly over apples. Bake in 375°F (190°C) oven for 25 to 30 minutes until top is browned and apples are tender.

Variations:

• Oatmeal Cranberry-Apple Crisp: Prepare 5 large apples; add 1 cup (250 mL) fresh or frozen cranberries.
• Oatmeal Apple-Peach Crisp: Prepare 4 large apples; add 4 to 5 fresh peeled and sliced peaches.
• Oatmeal Apple-Blueberry Crisp: Prepare 5 large apples; add 1 cup (250 mL) fresh or frozen unsweetened blueberries.

Substitute 2 tbsp (25 mL) white rum for the brandy.
• Three-Fruit Oatmeal Crisp: Prepare 3 large apples; add 4 fresh peeled and sliced peaches and 1 cup (250 mL) fresh or frozen unsweetened blueberries.

Pudding and Fruit

This is a simple idea and very easy to prepare. If served in fancy parfait glasses, it takes on a festive look.

1	pkg (4 oz/113 g) sugar-free instant vanilla pudding	1
1 cup	fresh or frozen unsweetened blueberries, sliced strawberries, sliced bananas, diced peaches or raspberries	250 mL

Follow directions on pudding package, using skim milk.

Blend in fruit with pudding, or layer alternately with pudding in 4 parfait glasses.

Refrigerate for 1 hour or longer before serving. Makes 4 servings.

Variation:
Any homemade stewed fruit — apples, peaches, pears, plums — can be used instead of fresh. In a hurry? Use well-drained unsweetened canned fruit.

Super Chunky Applesauce

Any variety of apples or a mixture may be used.

8 to 9 cups	peeled, sliced apples	2 to 2.25 L
1/3 cup	lemon juice	75 mL
2 tbsp	brandy (or 2 tsp/10 mL brandy extract)	25 mL
1/2 cup	orange juice	125 mL

½ cup	water	125 mL
⅓ cup	brown sugar or granulated sugar substitute	75 mL
2 tsp	cinnamon	10 mL

In large heavy pot, combine apples, lemon juice, brandy, orange juice, water and sugar. Cook over medium heat, stirring often until most of the apples have dissolved into sauce, but some remain in chunks. Remove sauce from heat; let cool for 15 to 20 minutes. Stir in cinnamon. Store sauce in containers; refrigerate.

This applesauce can be served warm or cold. Diet Whipped Topping (pg. 219) is very nice with this.

Pudding with Pears and Raspberry Sauce

This is a very elegant way to end a meal, or a wonderful cool dessert on a hot summer afternoon. It can be prepared the day before and assembled before serving. Canned whole or half pears may be used if they're packed in water (no sugar).

3	whole fresh pears	3
1	pkg (4 oz/113 g) sugar-free vanilla instant pudding	1
¾ to 1 cup	fresh or frozen unsweetened raspberries	175 to 250 mL
1 tbsp	cornstarch	15 mL
3 tbsp	cold water	50 mL
	Granulated sugar or liquid artificial sweetener	

Carefully peel the fresh pears; poach in boiling water just until they are tender. Remove from water; chill.

Slice each pear in half lengthwise; remove stem and hollow out center to remove seeds and create place to hold pudding. If using canned pears, chill can in refrigerator before use; remove pears from can, drain and dry with paper towel.

Prepare vanilla pudding following package directions but use skim milk. Let pudding chill and set in refrigerator before using.

In small saucepan, place raspberries and add enough water to cover. Cook over medium heat for 6 minutes until berries are very soft and mushy. Remove from heat; put raspberries through strainer. Discard raspberry seeds. Dissolve cornstarch in cold water; add to strained raspberries. Cook sauce over medium heat until thick, transparent and bubbly. Remove from heat; add granulated sugar to taste. Refrigerate to cool.

Assemble hours before or just before serving.

In each of 6 champagne glasses, place 1 pear half, cut side up. Into pear hollow where core had been, place 1/4 cup (50 mL) vanilla pudding. Drizzle with cold raspberry sauce. Extra sauce may be served at the table. Makes 6 servings.

Strawberries and Cream Mousse

2 cups	fresh strawberries	500 mL
3 tbsp	granulated sugar or powdered sugar substitute	50 mL
2 tbsp	orange brandy or 2 tsp/10 mL orange extract	25 mL
2 tsp	unflavored gelatin	10 mL
2 tbsp	cold water	25 mL
1/2 cup	instant skim-milk powder	125 mL
1/2 cup	ice water	125 mL
2 tbsp	granulated sugar	25 mL

In food processor or blender, purée half of the berries or enough to yield 1 cup (250 mL). Add sugar; blend. Slice remaining berries; combine in shallow bowl with brandy. Let stand for about 30 minutes.

Soften the gelatin in cold water; dissolve over low heat or in microwave oven. Stir into strawberry purée.

Whip skim-milk powder with ice water; add sugar. Whip until stiff peaks form. Fold strawberry purée and sliced strawberries into whipped milk. Turn into glass serving bowl; chill until firm.

Espresso Jelly

This delightful dessert is as easy as making gelatin; it can be made with brewed or instant espresso, or very strong brewed or instant coffee.

1/3 cup	granulated sugar or sugar substitute to taste	75 mL
2 cups	espresso or strong black coffee	500 mL
1	envelope (1 tbsp/15 mL) unflavored gelatin	1
3 tbsp	cold water	50 mL
	Diet Whipped Topping (pg. 219)	
	Shaved chocolate (optional)	
	Cinnamon	
	Granulated sugar	

Add sugar to hot coffee. (It will taste less sweet when it is chilled.) Stir gelatin into cold water; stir well into hot coffee until dissolved.

Pour into 6 dessert dishes or espresso cups. Chill until firm, about 2 hours. Before serving, top each dish with Diet Whipped Topping. Sprinkle with shaved chocolate (if using) and cinnamon mixed with granulated sugar. Makes 6 servings.

Variation:
Reduce coffee by ½ cup (125 mL). Mix into coffee ½ cup (125 mL) skim milk after gelatin has been dissolved.

Diet Whipped Topping

This versatile topping can be used on any dessert in the same way as whipped cream is used. This recipe is basic, but many flavorings may be used — even pure powdered cocoa can be added. Check the variation below for another way to serve this topping. This whipped topping is not as stable as whipped cream.

2 tsp	unflavored gelatin	10 mL
2 tbsp	cold water	25 mL
	Boiling water	
	Ice cubes	
½ cup	ice water	125 mL
¾ cup	skim-milk powder	175 mL
½ tsp	vanilla	2 mL
½ tsp	lemon juice	2 mL
2 tbsp	liquid honey or liquid sugar substitute equal to 3 tbsp (50 mL) sugar	25 mL

Dissolve gelatin in cold water. Add enough boiling water to gelatin to bring it up to ¼ cup (50 mL); stir until dissolved. Add enough ice cubes to bring level of water to ¾ cup (175 mL); let ice dissolve.

In small bowl of electric beater, mix ice water and skim-milk powder at medium speed. Add vanilla and lemon juice. Increase speed to high; add honey. While slowly adding gelatin, continue to whip until stiff peaks form, about 10 minutes.

This cream may be refrigerated until needed. It will be stable for about 1 hour. It can be re-whipped before using if it starts to wilt. Topping serves 6 to 8.

Variation:
On a piece of waxed paper, using a small spoon or pastry bag, place topping in circles to form 5 to 6 nests. Freeze nests for several hours. Fill with fruit, pudding or Espresso Jelly cubes. Serve shells still frozen.

Blueberry Grunt

This is a blueberry lover's delight. The recipe is classic — all that was needed was to reduce the sugar, salt and fat. I usually make this with fresh blueberries in season, but frozen unsweetened ones work just as well.

1⅓ cups	fresh or frozen unsweetened blueberries	325 mL
1½ cups	water	375 mL
½ cup	sugar or equivalent in liquid substitute	125 mL
	Grated rind from 1 lemon	
4 tsp	cornstarch	20 mL
¼ cup	water	50 mL
2 tbsp	white rum	25 mL
1½ cups	all-purpose flour	375 mL
2 tbsp	baking powder	25 mL
1 tbsp	cold margarine	15 mL
½ cup	skim milk	125 mL

In an 8-cup (2 L) pot, combine blueberries, 1½ cups (375 mL) water, sugar and lemon rind. Cook over medium heat. When blueberries start to cook, add cornstarch dissolved in ¼ cup (50 mL) water. Stir in white rum. Mix well; reduce heat to low. The blueberries should cook gently.

Meanwhile, in small bowl, mix together flour and baking powder.

Using pastry cutter or two knives, cut in margarine until mixture resembles coarse meal. Add milk to flour mixture, mixing just enough to moisten (do not overmix). Drop heaping tablespoon-size pieces of dough into pot of simmering blueberries. Cover pot; cook gently over low heat for 10 minutes. Serve dumplings with blueberries, warm or at room temperature. Makes 5 or 6 servings.

Graham Cracker Crust
(8- or 9-inch/20 cm or 23 cm)

1 cup	graham cracker crumbs	250 mL
3 tbsp	margarine, melted	50 mL
1½ tsp	granulated sugar (optional)	7 mL

In bowl, combine all ingredients. Press into bottom and sides of 8-inch (20 cm) or 9-inch (23 cm) pie plate, or into bottom only of 9-inch (2.5 L) springform pan.

For pie crust, bake in 400°F (200°C) oven for 5 minutes; for a refrigerator cheesecake, chill for 45 minutes before filling.

Variations:
Any one of the following may be used in place of the graham cracker crumbs, using the same recipe.

1 cup (250 mL) crushed crisp rice cereal
1 cup (250 mL) crushed bran flake cereal
1 cup (250 mL) crushed homemade Arrowroot
    Cookies (pg. 227)
1 cup (250 mL) crushed commercial arrowroot cookies
1 cup (250 mL) crushed cornflake cereal
1 cup (250 mL) 1-minute toasted oats
1 cup (250 mL) crushed Weetabix cereal

Note:
All of the ingredients for the graham crust and the variations may be used without sugar, as they all contain small amounts of sugar of their own. For those who like things sweeter, 1 tbsp (15 mL) sugar may be added. Before adding that sugar, though, consider the sweetness of the intended filling.

Oatmeal Tart Crust

1 cup	quick-cooking rolled oats	250 mL
1 cup	finely ground walnuts or almonds	250 mL
1	egg white	1
2 tbsp	frozen unsweetened apple juice concentrate, thawed	25 mL
½ tsp	cinnamon	2 mL

In bowl, blend all ingredients. Spray 9-inch (23 cm) tart pan or bottom of 9-inch (2.5 L) springform pan with vegetable spray. Place the mixture on bottom, pressing lightly. Bake in 375°F (190°C) oven for 6 to 8 minutes.

Country-Style Pie Dough

This recipe came from my mother. I remember her wonderful apple pies when I was a child. I have changed a few things to lower the calories, fat and sugar. It does not change the fine taste or texture. This dough is wonderful for Country-Style Apple Pie (pg. 223). It is so easy to make and handle, with perfect results all the time. I highly recommend this dough for novice pie makers.

2 cups	all-purpose flour	500 mL
⅓ cup	granulated sugar	75 mL
1 tbsp	baking powder	15 mL
⅓ cup	margarine (cold)	75 mL
1	egg (or 2 egg whites)	1
1 tsp	vanilla	5 mL
⅓ cup	low-fat (1%) yogurt	75 mL

In large bowl, combine flour, sugar and baking powder. Use pastry cutter or two knives to cut in margarine until mixture resembles coarse meal.

Beat egg; add vanilla and yogurt, mixing until blended. Add egg mixture to flour; use fork to blend. When this becomes difficult, turn dough out onto floured surface; knead.

This dough will be so soft and easy to handle that even an absolute beginner will have good results. It can be used immediately or refrigerated for several days or frozen for several months.

Before rolling out dough, dust some flour on the work surface to prevent sticking. This dough can be easily patched if you miscalculate the size or tear the dough. Bake according to the type of filling being used.

Country-Style Apple Pie

This is one of my family's favorites. I learned how to make this pie from my mother and went on to try new variations. My son is especially fond of this version.

	Country-Style Pie Dough (pg. 222)	
6 cups	peeled, sliced Spy or other baking apple	1.5 L
2 tbsp	cornstarch	25 mL
½ cup	orange juice	125 mL
2 tbsp	lemon juice	25 mL
⅓ cup	brown sugar or sugar substitute	75 mL
2 tbsp	brandy (or 2 tsp/(10 mL brandy extract)	25 mL
2 or 3 tsp	cinnamon	10 or 15 mL

For bottom crust, roll out half of the dough; place into 11- × 7-inch (2 L) glass baking dish. Trim away excess.

Place apple slices in large bowl. Mix cornstarch into orange juice; pour over apples, mixing to coat. Sprinkle apples with lemon juice, sugar, brandy and cinnamon. Mix well to coat all apples. Pour apples into prepared crust; distribute evenly. Apples should be piled high; they will shrink when baked.

Roll out remaining dough; place on top of apples. Seal

crusts around edges by folding excess dough under, applying a small amount of pressure. Crust will seal itself in baking. Make several slits in top crust to allow steam to escape.

Bake in 375°F (190°C) oven for 40 to 45 minutes until crust is well browned all over. Serve warm or cold.

Variations:

• Substitutes for brown sugar:

1. 3 to 4 tbsp (50 mL) Dried Fruit Spread (pg. 34) melted in ¼ cup (50 mL) dry white wine. (Omit brandy from pie recipe.)
2. 3 to 4 tbsp (50 mL) frozen unsweetened juice concentrate of apple, orange, lime or lemon
3. 3 to 4 tbsp (50 mL) liquid honey

• Apple-Peach Pie: Substitute fresh peaches for up to half of the apples. Instead of orange juice, substitute apple juice.

• Apple-Blueberry Pie: Substitute 1 to 1½ cups (250 mL to 375 mL) fresh or frozen unsweetened blueberries for equal amount of apples. Add 1 tbsp (15 mL) grated lemon peel. Substitute white rum for brandy.

• Cran-Apple Pie: Substitute 1 to 1½ cups (250 mL to 375 mL) fresh or frozen unsweetened cranberries for equal amount of apples. Substitute white rum for brandy. Add 1 tbsp (15 mL) grated orange rind.

• Apple-Pear Pie: Substitute 1 to 1½ cups (250 mL to 375 mL) fresh pears for an equal amount of apples. Substitute for the brown sugar 3 to 4 tbsp (50 mL) frozen raspberry juice concentrate, thawed.

Lemon Meringue Pie

This is as easy as the package mix; the real difference is the amount of sugar used. The flavor is terrific because of the fresh lemon.

1 cup	cold water	250 mL
½ cup	cornstarch	125 mL
½ cup	granulated sugar	125 mL
1½ cups	boiling water	375 mL
	Grated rind of 1 lemon	
½ cup	lemon juice	125 mL
2	egg yolks	2
1 tbsp	margarine	15 mL
2	egg whites	2
¼ tsp	cream of tartar	1 mL
⅓ cup	sugar	75 mL
1	baked pastry pie shell or unbaked crumb crust	1

In saucepan, combine cold water with cornstarch, mixing to blend. Add sugar and boiling water; stir well. Add lemon rind. Cook over low heat until mixture thickens.

Remove from heat; stir in lemon juice. Mix 3 tbsp (50 mL) of the hot mixture into the egg yolks to blend; then mix yolks into the saucepan. Cook over low heat for 2 to 3 minutes. Remove from heat; stir in margarine.

Let lemon filling cool until just warm. Fill pie shell.

Read "How To Make Perfect Meringue" (pg. 242). Using electric beater, whip egg whites; add cream of tartar and sugar. Beat until stiff peaks form. Spread over top of pie; place under broiler until lightly browned. Refrigerate until cold.

Cheese Apple Pie

You can vary the type of cheese used, which will affect the fat and calorie count, but fortunately not the quality, taste or visual effect.

Half	recipe Country-Style Pie Dough (pg. 222)	Half
3 cups	peeled, thinly sliced Spy or other baking apple	750 mL
1/4 tsp	cinnamon	1 mL
1/2 cup	orange juice	125 mL
1 tbsp	brandy (or 2 tsp/10 mL brandy extract)	15 mL
1 1/4 cup	skim milk	300 mL
1/2 cup	skim-milk powder	125 mL
2	large eggs (or 1 whole egg + 2 whites)	2
4 oz	light cream cheese or Skim-Milk Yogurt Cheese (pg. 72)	125 g
1 tsp	vanilla	5 mL
1/3 cup	granulated sugar	75 mL

Place dough in 10-inch (25 cm) pie plate. Trim excess; crimp top edge. Chill.

In a skillet, cook apples, cinnamon, orange juice and brandy, stirring occasionally until just tender. Drain, reserving liquid.   In glass measuring cup in microwave oven, or in a pot on top of stove, scald together skim milk and milk powder. Set aside to cool.

In bowl, beat together eggs with cheese. Add vanilla and sugar; beat well. Gradually beat in cooled milk and reserved juice from apples.

Spread apples in bottom of chilled crust. Pour cheese mixture over apples, filling pie to crimped top. Bake in 350°F (180°C) oven for 45 to 50 minutes until knife inserted in middle comes out clean. Let cool before serving.

Cookies and Cakes to Remember

Arrowroot Cookies

This cookie can be changed by varying the flavorings.

½ cup	margarine (at room temperature)	125 mL
½ cup	granulated sugar	125 mL
1 tsp	vanilla	5 mL
1 tbsp	brandy (or 2 tsp/10 mL brandy extract)	15 mL
¼ cup	water	50 mL
1 tsp	baking powder	5 mL
1¼ cups	all-purpose flour	300 mL
1 cup	arrowroot flour	250 mL

In large bowl, using electric mixer, beat together margarine, sugar, vanilla and brandy until well blended and fluffy, about 5 minutes. Add water slowly, mixing as it is added. Beat for an additional minute.

Blend baking powder into all-purpose flour; add to creamed mixture. Using large spoon, mix until flour is totally blended. Add arrowroot flour, using spoon to mix until it becomes difficult.

Using your hands, knead dough until quite smooth. Divide in half; roll very thin (less than ¼ inch/5 mm).

Using your favorite cookie cutters, cut cookies. Place close together on cookie sheets sprayed with vegetable spray. Bake in 350°F (180°C) oven for 10 to 12 minutes or until lightly browned.

Makes about 40 small cookies.

Variation:
Add ¼ cup (50 mL) poppy seeds to all-purpose flour.

Oat Bran Shortbread Cookies

This is a terrific shortbread cookie with the added nutrition of oat bran. This recipe will not disappoint you.

⅓ cup	margarine (at room temperature)	75 mL
½ cup	brown sugar	125 mL
2 tbsp	mayonnaise	25 mL
1 tsp	almond flavoring	5 mL
1 tbsp	grated lemon peel	15 mL
½ cup	oat bran	125 mL
1¼ cups	all-purpose flour	300 mL
1 tsp	baking soda	5 mL

In large mixing bowl, using electric mixer, cream together margarine, sugar, mayonnaise, almond flavoring and lemon peel. Beat until light and fluffy, about 5 minutes. Add oat bran; mix well. Combine all-purpose flour and baking soda; mix into batter with large spoon.

Chill dough for 1 hour. Roll out on floured surface to ¼-inch (5 mm) thickness. Use small round or square cookie cutter to cut. Bake on ungreased cookie sheets in 325° (160°C) oven for 20 to 25 minutes until lightly browned. Makes 3 dozen cookies.

Chinese Almond Cookies

These cookies were adapted from a real Chinese recipe. The texture is excellent and the flavor is as good as its original high-sugar, high-fat and high-calorie counterpart.

½ cup	margarine (at room temperature)	125 mL
½ cup	granulated sugar	125 mL
1	egg	1
2 tsp	almond extract	10 mL
½ cup	ground blanched almonds	125 mL
2 cups	all-purpose flour	500 mL
2 tbsp	cornstarch	25 mL
1½ tsp	baking powder	7 mL

36	blanched almond halves (optional)	36
1	egg white	1
1 tbsp	water	15 mL

In large mixing bowl, using electric mixer, cream margarine, sugar, egg and almond extract until light and fluffy, about 5 minutes. Add ground almonds, mixing well.

Blend flour, cornstarch and baking powder; add to creamed mixture, using large spoon to mix until dough is formed. Use your hands to mix, using gentle kneading action.

Shape dough into 36 small balls; place on ungreased cookie sheets. Place one almond half on each ball; flatten with the palm of your hand.

Mix egg white with water; brush glaze over each cookie. Bake in 350°F (180°C) oven for 20 minutes or until golden; do not allow cookies to brown. Makes 36 cookies.

Chocolate Chip Cookies

This is a reduced sugar and fat version of the classic chewy chocolate chip cookie. My children really think it stacks up.

⅓ cup	margarine (at room temperature)	75 mL
3 tbsp	mayonnaise	50 mL
1 cup	(not packed) brown sugar	250 mL
1	egg	1
2 tsp	vanilla	10 mL
1 tbsp	lemon juice	15 mL
3 tbsp	low-fat (1%) yogurt	50 mL
½ tsp	baking soda	2 mL
2 cups	all-purpose flour	500 mL
½ cup	mini chocolate chips	125 mL

In a large bowl, using electric mixer, cream together margarine, mayonnaise and brown sugar; beat until blended. Add egg, lemon juice, yogurt and vanilla. Continue to beat at high speed for 5 minutes until thick and fluffy.

Stir together baking soda and flour. Beat 1 cup flour mixture into creamed mixture. Stir in remaining flour and chocolate chips.

Break off small pieces of dough the size of a walnut; roll into balls and flatten very thin on ungreased cookie sheets. Bake in 375°F (190°C) oven for 10 to 12 minutes until browned. Makes about 40 cookies.

Variations:

- Any type of chips may be substituted for chocolate.
- ¼ cup (50 mL) chopped walnuts may be added with the chips. However, they will add fat and calories; if that is a concern, try ⅓ cup (75 mL) roasted large-flake oatmeal.
- For an almond chocolate chip cookie, slivered almonds may be added; substitute almond flavoring for the vanilla. When the almond flavor is wanted without the added fat and calories of nuts, just substitute pure almond flavoring for the vanilla.
- Oatmeal Chocolate Chip: Reduce flour by 1 cup (250 mL) and add 1 cup (250 mL) regular rolled oats.
- Chocolate Chocolate Chip: Add to the creamed mixture ¼ cup (50 mL) pure unsweetened cocoa. Slightly more liquid will be needed: add 2 or 3 tbsp (25 mL or 50 mL) skim milk.

Chocolate Refrigerator Cookies

This cookie has a very satisfying chocolate taste. It can be made into long rolls, refrigerated for many days before baking or frozen for many months and baked fresh at any time.

½ cup	margarine (at room temperature)	125 mL
½ cup	brown sugar	125 mL
3 tbsp	pineapple juice concentrate	50 mL
1 tsp	vanilla	5 mL
1 tsp	vinegar	5 mL

1 tbsp	instant coffee dissolved in 1 tbsp (15 mL) boiling water	15 mL
6 tbsp	cocoa powder	90 mL
1³/₄ cups	all-purpose flour	425 mL

In large bowl, using electric mixer, beat together margarine, brown sugar, pineapple juice, vanilla and vinegar until thick and fluffy. Slowly add coffee mixed with water; beat to mix.

Add cocoa; beat until blended and creamy. Gradually stir in flour with a large spoon until dough forms.

On lightly floured surface, shape dough into two 9-inch (23 cm) rolls. Wrap in waxed paper and chill in refrigerator for 2 hours (or 45 minutes in freezer) before baking.

Slice rolls into ¼-inch (5 mm) slices; place on ungreased cookie sheets. Bake in 350°F (180°C) oven for 12 minutes. Makes 36 to 40 cookies.

Variations:
• This dough can be rolled into a flat rectangle and rolled up with the Orange Pinwheel Cookie dough (pg. 234) to make Chocolate Orange Pinwheel Cookies.
• Substitute pure almond flavoring for the vanilla; place half an almond on top of each chocolate cookie.

Butter Cookies

Don't let the name fool you — there is no butter in these cookies, yet they taste as rich and buttery as their high-cholesterol counterpart.

¹/₃ cup	margarine (at room temperature)	75 mL
4 oz	light cream cheese	125 g
³/₄ cup	granulated sugar	175 mL
1 tsp	almond flavoring	5 mL
1 tbsp	lemon juice concentrate	15 mL
1	egg + 1 egg white	1

| 2¼ cups | all-purpose flour | 550 mL |
| 1 tsp | baking powder | 5 mL |

Topping:

| ¼ cup | brown sugar | 50 mL |
| 1 tsp | cinnamon | 5 mL |

In large bowl, using electric mixer, beat margarine, cream cheese, sugar, almond flavoring, lemon juice and eggs until light and fluffy, about 5 minutes.

Blend flour with baking powder; add to creamed mixture, using large spoon to mix until soft dough forms.

Divide dough into 2 portions; shape each into a roll. Stir together well brown sugar and cinnamon; sprinkle over sheet of waxed paper. Roll each cookie roll in cinnamon mixture to coat well. Wrap each roll separately in waxed paper and refrigerate for 2 hours. Dough can be left in refrigerator for several days or frozen for several months.

Slice rolls into ¼-inch (5 mm) slices; place 1 inch (2.5 cm) apart on cookie sheets sprayed with vegetable spray. Bake in 350°F (180°C) oven for about 12 minutes. Makes 50 cookies.

Shortbread Cookies

This is a very old recipe passed on to my mother and then to me. I have changed it only to reduce fat and sugar. Nevertheless, the cookies still are a tribute to the relative who was known for them.

1	whole egg + 3 egg whites	1
1 cup	(scant) granulated sugar	250 mL
1½ cups	margarine (at room temperature)	375 mL
2 tbsp	canola oil	25 mL
2 tsp	vanilla	10 mL
1 tbsp	grated lemon rind	15 mL
4½ cups	all-purpose flour	1.125 L

3 tbsp	baking powder	50 mL
	Crushed walnuts	
	Cinnamon	
	Crushed roasted oatmeal	
	Granulated sugar	

In large bowl, using electric mixer, beat together eggs, sugar, margarine, oil, vanilla and lemon rind, 10 to 12 minutes.

In separate bowl, combine flour and baking powder. Add half of the flour mixture to creamed mixture; beat well.

Add remaining flour, mixing with large spoon until well blended. Place dough in bowl, tightly cover with plastic wrap and refrigerate overnight. Cookie dough can be rolled and cut into any desired shape. Make dough into small cookie rolls, about 1½ inches (4 cm) in diameter. Wrap each roll in waxed paper and freeze in plastic bags.

The next day, divide dough into four pieces. Roll out one piece at a time on lightly floured surface. Roll to ¼-inch (5 mm) thickness; use very small cookie cutters to cut cookies. Tops can be left plain or pressed into dish of crushed walnuts with cinnamon; cinnamon mixed with crushed roasted oatmeal; or cinnamon-sugar mixture.

Place cookies close together on ungreased baking sheet. Bake in 350°F (180°C) oven for about 20 minutes. Watch that they do not brown.

Cool on rack; store in tightly covered tin. Makes about 80 cookies.

Meringue Cookies

Light and crisp, these cookies are classic. Follow the directions for making perfect meringue (pg. 242). Here's a tip: separate yolks from whites while eggs are cold.

3	egg whites (at room temperature)	3
1 tsp	cream of tartar	5 mL
9 tbsp	granulated sugar	135 mL

½ tsp	vanilla extract	2 mL
½ tsp	brandy (optional)	2 mL
½ cup	mini chocolate chips or chopped walnuts or combination	125 mL

Beat egg whites until foamy; add cream of tartar. Add sugar, 1 tbsp (15 mL) at a time, with vanilla and brandy (if using) being added halfway through sugar additions. Beat meringue until stiff glossy peaks form. Fold in chocolate chips.

Drop batter by teaspoonfuls (5 mL) onto cookie sheet sprayed with vegetable spray. Bake in 225°F (100°C) oven for 1½ hours. Turn oven off; let cookies cool in oven with door ajar for 1 hour.

Remove with metal spatula; store in airtight container.

Orange Pinwheel Cookies

These cookies can be made many ways depending upon personal tastes. I have included a list of choices for the filling; the basic cookie remains the same.

1½ cups	all-purpose flour	375 mL
1 tsp	baking powder	5 mL
⅓ cup	margarine (at room temperature)	75 mL
½ cup	unsweetened orange juice Filling (see *Variations*)	125 mL

In large mixing bowl, blend together flour and baking powder.

Using two knives or pastry cutter, cut in margarine until mixture resembles coarse meal. Add orange juice, using spoon to mix until dough forms. Using your hands, knead dough until it holds together.

Remove dough to lightly floured surface. Knead for 1 to 2 minutes; then roll out using flour to prevent sticking. Roll dough into rectangle. Cover surface with one of the fillings listed below.

Roll dough in jelly-roll fashion from the long edge. Refrigerate for several hours or freeze for 45 minutes. Slice ¼ inch (5 mm) thick; place on ungreased cookie sheet. Bake in 450°F (230°C) oven for 12 minutes.

Variations:
- Spread ¼ cup (50 mL) Dried Fruit Spread (pg. 34) over the dough before rolling.
- Spread cinnamon and sugar over dough before rolling.
- Sprinkle ¼ cup (50 mL) mini chocolate chips or butterscotch chips over dough before rolling.
- Brush 4 to 5 tbsp (50 mL to 75 mL) unsweetened raspberry, strawberry, blueberry or grape jam over dough (use pastry brush) before rolling.

Marble Coffee Cake

My mother made this cake when I was a child; however, her version had more sugar and fat. I have retained the same great taste and texture, but removed many calories, fat and half of the sugar. A word of caution: FOLLOW THE DIRECTIONS!

⅓ cup	margarine (at room temperature)	75 mL
½ cup	granulated sugar	125 mL
2	large eggs (or 1 whole egg + 2 whites)	2
1 tsp	vanilla	5 mL
2 tsp	lemon juice	10 mL
2 cups	all-purpose flour	500 mL
3 tbsp	baking powder	50 mL
1 cup	low-fat (1%) yogurt	250 mL
1 tsp	baking soda	5 mL
⅓ cup	cocoa powder	75 mL

2 tbsp	canola oil	25 mL
2 tsp	(approx) cinnamon	10 mL
¼ cup	(approx) brown sugar	50 mL

In large mixing bowl, using electric mixer, beat margarine, sugar, eggs and vanilla. Add lemon juice about 3 to 4 minutes into the beating. Beat about 5 minutes, until batter is very thick and fluffy.

In 2-cup (500 mL) measure, blend flour with baking powder. Blend yogurt with baking soda. When yogurt foams, pour half of it into creamed mixture. Add half of the flour mixture to creamed mixture. Beat well. Add remaining flour and yogurt, beating well. The batter will be thick, but it is important that it be beaten well. Pour batter into 9-inch (2.5 L) square cake pan lined with aluminum foil.

In drinking glass, mix together cocoa and oil until blended and smooth. Pour chocolate over batter, using spatula or knife to swirl chocolate into batter. Using spatula or knife, level out top of cake. Sprinkle with cinnamon and brown sugar. Bake in 375°F (190°C) oven for 30 to 35 minutes. Test for doneness with wooden toothpick.

Variation:
Add to the topping several roughly crushed cookies (any type). The brown sugar may be partially reduced or omitted if using the crushed cookies.

Saucepan Chocolate Brownies

These brownies are as fast and easy as any commercial brownie mix, and even with the sugar and fat reduced they taste terrific. Eat them plain or sprinkled with icing sugar. For a special treat try the easy Basic Icing that follows.

2 tbsp	canola oil	25 mL
⅔ cup	granulated sugar	150 mL
2 tbsp	concentrated orange or lemon juice	25 mL
6 tbsp	unsweetened cocoa powder	90 mL
1	egg white	1
1 tsp	vanilla	5 mL
1 tbsp	Kahlua (optional)	15 mL
⅔ cup	all-purpose flour	150 mL
½ tsp	baking soda	2 mL

In medium saucepan over low heat, cook canola oil, sugar and orange juice, stirring constantly until sugar is melted. Add cocoa powder; stir until well blended. Remove from heat. In small bowl, lightly beat egg white with vanilla and Kahlua. Stir into chocolate mixture until well blended.

Combine flour and baking soda; stir into chocolate mixture to blend well. Batter will be very thick. Scrape batter into 9-inch (2.5 L) square baking pan well coated with vegetable spray, spreading evenly over pan. Bake in 350°F (180°C) oven for 15 minutes. Be careful not to overbake; the brownie should show moisture on a toothpick when tested.

Variations:
• Add ⅓ to ½ cup (75 mL to 125 mL) chopped nuts. (To control calories *and* enjoy a nutty flavor, add ½ tsp (2 mL) almond flavoring.)
• Basic Icing: In small bowl, mix together ⅔ cup (150 mL) icing sugar, 1 to 2 tbsp (15 mL to 25 mL) unsweetened cocoa, 1 tbsp (15 mL) margarine (at room temperature), 1 tsp (5 mL) vanilla and enough water to moisten mixture; beat, using electric mixer, until thick and creamy. If too thick, add a drop or two of water; if too thin, add 1 or 2 tbsp (15 mL to 25 mL) icing sugar.
• You can substitute for the margarine 2 tbsp (25 mL) light cream cheese (at room temperature) and 1 tbsp (15 mL) low-fat yogurt; reduce amount of water.

Bavarian Apple Torte

I have been making this torte for many years. It never fails to receive raves from everyone. Not only does it taste great, but it has a very finished and professional look that will enhance any occasion.

¼ cup	margarine (cold)	50 mL
2 tbsp	granulated sugar	25 mL
¼ tsp	vanilla	1 mL
¾ cup	all-purpose flour	175 mL
8 oz	light cream cheese or Skim-Milk Yogurt Cheese (pg. 72), well drained and very thick	250 g
1 tsp	vanilla	5 mL
1 tsp	grated lemon rind	5 mL
1	egg (or 2 egg whites)	1
4 cups	peeled, thinly sliced Spy or other baking apples	1 L
¼ cup	granulated sugar	50 mL
1 tsp	cinnamon	5 mL
1 tsp	lemon juice	5 mL
1 tbsp	brandy (or 2 tsp/10 mL brandy extract)	15 mL
¼ cup	slivered almonds (optional)	50 mL

To make crust, in small bowl, beat margarine, sugar and ¼ tsp (1 mL) vanilla until well blended. Stir in flour until mixture forms soft dough. Press dough into bottom and about 1½ inches (4 cm) up side of ungreased 9-inch (2.5 L) springform pan.

In bowl, using electric mixer, beat together cream cheese, 1 tsp (5 mL) vanilla, lemon rind and egg until smooth. Pour into springform pan.

In bowl, combine apples, sugar, cinnamon, lemon juice and brandy. Mix well until all apples are well coated.

Starting along outside edge of pan, arrange apples in a ring, with the rounded outside edges facing up and with slices pointing towards center. Arrange a ring in the center of the pan, then fill remaining space with remaining slices. Sprinkle almonds (if using) on top.

Bake in 450°F (230°C) oven for 10 minutes; lower heat to 400°F (200°C) and bake 25 minutes longer. Let cool in pan on wire rack before removing side. Serve at room temperature or chilled.

Banana-Bran Loaf

Simple to make, this loaf is a great way to use up old bananas. Slice it when cool. Try a slice in the toaster oven.

2 cups	all-purpose flour	500 mL
2 tbsp	baking powder	25 mL
¾ cup	skim milk	175 mL
1 cup	all-bran	250 mL
⅓ cup	margarine (at room temperature)	75 mL
⅓ cup	granulated sugar	75 mL
1	whole egg (or 2 egg whites)	1
1 tbsp	Cointreau (optional)	15 mL
2 tbsp	orange juice concentrate	25 mL
1 tbsp	cocoa powder	15 mL
2	very ripe large bananas, mashed	2
½ tsp	baking soda	2 mL
½ cup	low-fat (1%) yogurt	125 mL

Measure flour in 2-cup (500 mL) measuring cup; add baking powder. Mix well. Pour milk over all-bran; let stand to absorb all liquid.

In large bowl, with electric mixer, cream margarine, sugar and egg for 5 minutes, until light and fluffy. Add Cointreau (if using), orange juice and cocoa powder, beating well for another minute. Add bananas and bran mixture, beating until well blended.

Mix baking soda into yogurt; let it foam up. Add half of the flour mixture and half of the foaming yogurt to creamed mixture. Beat until blended; add remaining yogurt and flour, beating well. Turn mixture into loaf pan sprayed with vegetable spray. Bake in 375°F (190°C) oven for about 1 hour.

Variations:
½ cup (125 mL) of any of the following can be added to the batter after mixing in the flour and yogurt (remember, it will also change the sugar and calorie count): fresh cranberries, fresh or frozen unsweetened blueberries, chopped dried apricots, grated apple, raisins, chopped walnuts.

Useful Information

Some Special Equivalents

For all the years that I have been cooking (and I must admit they are adding up), one of the most frustrating experiences is to be confronted with unusual terms in measurement.

Things like a tumbler, gill, wine-glass full. Even recipes that call for a ½ lb of sugar can throw anyone used to the measurement appearing in cups. To add to the confusion, we are also dealing with metric.

I hope the following information that I have gathered over the years will assist you in decoding strange measurements that we see from time to time. I have included some other practical information that will help when making substitutions and answering certain questions (like how many marshmallows equal 1 cup.)

1 egg = 3 tbsp = 2 oz = 50 mL
1 egg yolk = 1 tbsp = 1 oz = 15 mL
1 egg white = 2 tbsp = 1 oz = 25 mL
8 to 10 egg whites = 1 cup = 250 mL
9 eggs = 1 lb = 500 g

1 cup (250 mL) granulated sugar = 6½ oz (165 g)
1 lb (500 g) granulated sugar = 2 cups (500 mL)
1 oz (50 g) granulated sugar = 2 tbsp (25 mL)
1 lb (500 g) icing sugar = 3½ cups (875 mL)
1 lb (500 g) brown sugar = 2¼ cups (550 mL) (packed)

4 tbsp (50 mL) flour = 1 oz (25 g)
1 lb (500 g) all-purpose flour = 4 cups (1 L)
1 lb (500 g) cake flour = 4½ cups (1.12 L)
1 cup (250 mL) cake flour = 1 cup less 2 tbsp (⅞ cup/225 mL)
    all-purpose flour
1 cup (250 mL) white all-purpose flour =
        1¼ cups (300 mL) rye flour = 300 mL
        ⅝ cup (160 mL) potato flour = 160 mL
        1 cup less 2 tbsp (⅞ cup/225 mL) rice flour

1 lb (500 g) margarine = 2 cups (500 mL)
16 tbsp margarine = 1 cup (250 mL)
4 tbsp margarine = ¼ cup (50 mL)

3 tbsp (50 mL) cocoa + 1 tbsp (15 mL) fat = 1 oz (28 g)
  unsweetened chocolate
4 cups (1 L) cocoa = 1 lb (500 g)
1 square chocolate = ¼ cup (50 mL) grated

1 lemon = 2 tbsp (25 mL) rind and 3 tbsp (50 mL) juice
1 orange = 2 tbsp (25 mL) rind and ½ cup (125 mL) juice
1 tsp (5 mL) grated rind = ½ tsp (2 mL) lemon extract
3 cups (750 mL) raisins = 1 lb (500 g)
8 oz (250 g) marshmallows = 32 large = 3¼ cups (800 mL)
  mini

1 envelope gelatin = 1 tbsp (15 mL)
1 envelope will gel 2 cups (500 mL) liquid
1 envelope dry granular yeast = 1 tbsp (15 mL)

1 tbsp (15 mL) fresh grated horseradish = 2 tbsp (25 mL)
  prepared

1 lb (500 g) cottage cheese = 2 cups (500 mL)
2 oz (50 g) grated cheese = ½ cup (125 mL)
1 lb (500 g) Cheddar = 4 to 5 cups (1 L to 1.25 L) grated

12 graham wafers = 1 cup (250 mL) finely ground
1 slice bread = ¼ cup (50 mL) dry = ½ cup (125 mL) soft
  bread crumbs

1 gill = 8 tbsp = ½ cup (125 mL)
1 tumbler = 1 cup (250 mL)
1 wine-glass = ¼ cup (50 mL)
1 dessert spoon = 2 tsp (10 mL)

How to Make Perfect Meringue

1. Always start with COLD eggs. It is easier to separate the white from the yolk when the egg is cold from the refrigerator. Be careful when separating; even a trace of yolk can prevent the whites from whipping properly. After cracking the egg, let the white fall into a small dish. If the separation is successful, pour the white into the mixing bowl and do the next egg. If you have a broken yolk, store the egg in the refrigerator and use it for another purpose.

2. Egg whites should be placed in a glass or stainless-steel bowl, never aluminum, and never plastic. The oils in the plastic will inhibit the formation of the meringue, and the aluminum will react and give the whites a gray color. Let the whites stand for 30 minutes to 1 hour until they are at room temperature, and they will beat to a much higher volume.

3. Beat the whites until they are foamy before adding sugar. Sugar should be added gradually, 1 tbsp (15 mL) at a time so it will dissolve completely to avoid "beading" (small liquid beads on the surface of the meringue.)

4. Beat until meringue forms stiff glossy peaks. To test if the sugar is dissolved, rub some meringue between your fingers. If it feels grainy, continue beating until it feels smooth. This is the reason for adding the sugar at the foamy stage to avoid over-beating.

5. Spread meringue over warm filling to prevent weeping (forming liquid between the meringue and the filling). Meringue will weep if spread on a cooled filling.

6. Spread the meringue over the filling by starting all around the edge of the crust. Be sure to seal the meringue to the edge to prevent it from pulling away from the crust as it bakes. Use a dessert spoon to shape the meringue into peaks (not too high) and swirls.

7. Meringue should be baked in 350°F (180°C) oven for 12 to 15 minutes or until lightly browned, when being used on top of a pie. If it is baked either at too high a temperature or for too long, it will develop a tough chewy skin.

Soft Meringue (pies and baked desserts)
Ratio: 2 tbsp (25 mL) sugar per 1 egg white

Hard Meringue (cookies and dessert shells)
Ratio: 3 tbsp (50 mL) sugar per 1 egg white

If too much sugar is used the shells will be sticky. Bake in 225°F (100°C) oven for 1½ hours; let cool in the oven for 1 hour.

Thickening Liquids

Many types of thickeners can be used with liquids. The choice should be made depending on the finished results that are required. The following is a guide.

All-Purpose Flour
Thin Sauce: 1 tbsp (15 mL) flour per 1 cup (250 mL) liquid
Medium Sauce: 2 tbsp (25 mL) flour per 1 cup (250 mL) liquid
Thick Sauce: 3 tbsp (50 mL) flour per 1 cup (250 mL) liquid

Instant-blending flour is easier to work with, but if regular flour is dissolved first in cold water, then added slowly to the hot liquid, it will not become lumpy.

The thickening power of flour is reduced when:
• the flour is browned first;
• the flour is added to acidic foods (vinegar, lemon juice, wine or tomatoes);
• there is a large amount of sugar in the liquid;
• the liquid is overcooked.

Cornstarch
Ratio: 1 tbsp (15 mL) cornstarch is equal to 2 tbsp (25 mL) all-purpose flour
   The mixture will thicken as it cools; the liquid will have a glazed translucent appearance.
   The thickening power is reduced by acid and large amounts of sugar.

Tapioca
When used for thickening pudding, 4 tsp (20 mL) per cup (250 mL) of liquid

When used for fruit pie filling, 4 tsp to 3 tbsp (20 mL to 50 mL) for an 8- to 9-inch (20 cm to 23 cm) pie.

Arrowroot
Ratio: 1 tbsp (15 mL) is equal to 2 tbsp (25 mL) all-purpose flour
The liquid will have a translucent appearance and will thin if stirred too much.

Custard
The usual ratio is 1 egg plus 1 tsp (5 mL) sugar per 1 cup (250 mL) low-fat milk. More sugar makes the custard less firm and increases the cooking time. More eggs makes the custard more firm and shortens the cooking time.
   Stirred custard is soft; baked is more firm.

Miscellaneous

• To prevent yogurt from curdling, add it to other ingredients at the end of cooking time.
• Blend cornstarch with yogurt: 1 tsp (5 mL) cornstarch to ½ cup (125 mL) yogurt. This will stabilize yogurt when it is being heated.
• To remove the zest from a lemon, orange or lime, use a vegetable peeler. The peel can be frozen or dried and stored in a small jar.
• When substituting:
   1 cup (250 mL) margarine = ⅞ cup (225 mL) liquid oil
   1 cup (250 mL) shortening = ⅔ cup (150 mL) liquid oil
• When using wine for cooking, 85% of the calories and all the alcohol cooks off at 175°F (79°C).
• To whiten coffee or tea, try instant skim-milk powder. It contains no preservatives or sugar, is fat-free, shelf-stable and inexpensive compared with powdered creamers.

METRIC EQUIVALENTS

Metric Equivalents for Oven Temperatures

Fahrenheit	Celsius	Fahrenheit	Celsius
250°F	120°C	400°F	200°C
275°F	140°C	425°F	220°C
300°F	150°C	450°F	230°C
325°F	160°C	475°F	240°C
350°F	180°C	500°F	260°C
375°F	190°C	550°F	290°C

Metric Equivalents for Volume and Weight

Volume Measure	Metric Equivalent
¼ tsp	1 mL
½ tsp	2 mL
1 tsp	5 mL
1 tbsp (3 tsp)	15 mL
2 tbsp (1 fluid oz)	25 mL
¼ cup (4 tbsp) (2 fluid oz)	50 mL
⅓ cup	75 mL
½ cup (8 tbsp) (4 fluid oz)	125 mL
⅔ cup	150 mL
¾ cup (6 fluid oz)	175 mL
1 cup (8 fluid oz)	250 mL
1 pint (2 cups)	500 mL
1 quart (4 cups)	1 L

Weight Measure	Metric Equivalent
1 oz	25 g
2 oz	50 g
3 oz	75 g
¼ lb (4 oz)	125 g
½ lb (8 oz)	250 g
¾ lb (12 oz)	375 g
1 lb (16 ounces)	500 g

Metric Equivalents for Dimensions

½ inch .... 1 cm	4 inches .... 10 cm
1 inch .... 2.5 cm	5 inches .... 12 cm
1½ inches .... 4 cm	9 inches .... 23 cm
2 inches .... 5 cm	11 inches .... 28 cm
3 inches .... 8 cm	13 inches .... 33 cm

METRICATION

Solid and Dry Ingredients

Imperial	Approx. g to nearest whole figure	Recommended equivalent
½ oz	14 g	15 g
1	28	25
1½	42	40
2	57	50
3	85	75
4 (¼ lb)	113	125
5	142	150
6	170	175
7	198	200
8 (½ lb)	227	250
9	255	280
10	283	310
11	312	350
12 (¾ lb)	340	375
13	368	410
14	397	440
15	425	470
16 (1 lb)	454	500

Liquid and Fluid Ingredients

Imperial	Approx. mL to nearest whole figure	Recommended equivalent
2 fl oz (3 tbsp)	57 mL	50 mL
4 (6 tbsp)	113	100
5 (¼ pt)	142	150
6	170	175
7	198	200
8	227	225
9	255	250
10 (½ pt)	283	300
11	312	325
12	340	350
13	368	375
14	397	400
15 (¾ pt)	425	450
18	510	500(.5 L)
20 (1 pt)	567	600
1¼ pints	709	750
1½ pints	851	900
1¾ pints	992	1 L

Bibliography

Kraus, Barbara. *Calories and Carbohydrates.* 7th ed. New York: Plume/New American Library, 1987.

Jacobson, Dr. Michael, Bonnie F. Liebman, and Greg Moyer. *Salt: The Brand Name Guide to Sodium Content.* New York: Workman Publishing, 1983.

Diabetes Forecast. Alexandria, VA: The American Diabetes Association. Published monthly.

Diabetes Self-Management. New York: R.A. Rapaport Publishing. Published monthly.

Diabetes in the News. South Bend, IN: Ames Center for Diabetes Education, Miles Inc. Diagnostic Division, 224 E. Monroe. Published monthly.

Index